OTHER LEADERSHIP TITLES FROM
ROWMAN & LITTLEFIELD EDUCATION

A Path to Leadership: The Heroic Follower. Robert Palestini. 2006.

Celebrate Leadership: Lessons for Middle School Students. Maggie Meyer and Jenna Glock. 2006.

Leadership Mentoring: Maintaining School Improvement in Turbulent Times. Steven Jay Gross. 2006.

Priority Leadership: Generating School and District Improvement through Systemic Change. Robert T. Hess and James W. Robinson. 2006.

Qualities for Effective Leadership: School Leaders Speak. E. E. (Gene) Davis, ed. 2006.

5 Essential Skills of School Leadership: Moving from Good to Great. Nancy Langley and Mark Jacobs. 2005.

Instructional Leadership for Systemic Change: The Story of San Diego's Reform. Linda Darling-Hammond, Amy M. Hightower, Jennifer L. Husbands, Jeanette R. LaFors, Viki M. Young, and Carl Christopher. 2005.

Power, Politics, and Ethics in School Districts: Dynamic Leadership for Systemic Change. Francis M. Duffy. 2005.

Soft Leadership for Hard Times. George A. Goens. 2005.

The Art of Leadership: A Choreography of Human Understanding. Zach Kelehear. 2005.

The Cognitive Leader: Building Winning Organizations through Knowledge Leadership. Roderic Hewlett. 2005.

Educational Leadership: Knowing the Way, Going the Way, Showing the Way. Carolyn S. Carr and Connie L. Fulmer, eds. 2004.

Curriculum Leadership: Beyond Boilerplate Standards. Leo H. Bradley. 2003.

Standards-Based Leadership: A Case Study Book for the Principalship. Sandra Harris and Sandra Lowery. 2003.

The Expert
School Leader

Accelerating Accountability

Naftaly S. Glasman
and Lynette D. Glasman

ROWMAN & LITTLEFIELD EDUCATION
Lanham • New York • Toronto • Plymouth, UK

Published in the United States of America
by Rowman & Littlefield Education
A Division of Rowman & Littlefield Publishers, Inc.
A wholly owned subsidiary of The Rowman & Littlefield Publishing Group, Inc.
4501 Forbes Boulevard, Suite 200, Lanham, Maryland 20706
www.rowmaneducation.com

Estover Road
Plymouth PL6 7PY
United Kingdom

British Library Cataloguing in Publication Information Available

Library of Congress Cataloging-in-Publication Data

Glasman, Naftaly S., 1938–
  The expert school leader : accelerating accountability / Naftaly S. Glasman and
Lynette D. Glasman.
    p. cm.
  Includes bibliographical references.
  ISBN-13: 978-1-57886-525-3 (cloth : alk. paper)
  ISBN-13: 978-1-57886-526-0 (pbk. : alk. paper)
  ISBN-10: 1-57886-525-5 (cloth : alk. paper)
  ISBN-10: 1-57886-526-3 (pbk. : alk. paper)
  1. School management and organization. 2. Leadership. I. Glasman, Lynette D.,
1940– II. Title. LB2805.G533 2007
  371.2'011—dc22   2006020721

Manufactured in the United States of America.

Contents

Part III: Surveying School Leaders

**Part IV   Lessons: How to Improve
             School-Leadership Accountability**

Acknowledgments

Years of leadership practice, research, writing, and teaching have brought us together with numerous professional and lay individuals. They coached us, and they critiqued and improved our work. Their influence is evidenced in this book. We cannot thank them individually, but we thank them collectively. Most of these individuals were our own students. From them we learned the most. To them we owe special thanks.

Our eight interviewees taught us what for us were new ways of viewing school leadership and school-leadership accountability. With their help we were able to go with confidence out of the box and ask questions we had never asked before. We are so grateful to them for their time, openness, and wisdom.

We were fortunate to receive permission from two school superintendents and two school boards of education to survey busy professional educators who serve as school leaders in their districts. We were even more fortunate to receive from the eighty-two school leaders their responses to our long questionnaires.

The practicing school leaders helped us to reenter the box with confidence and check out their opinions about the recommendations offered by the external professionals. We sincerely appreciate the time and the information that they shared with us. The critiques that a few of them made about some of our questions were particularly beneficial.

Carol Glasman helped us with compiling and analyzing the survey data. She did it with great skill. Jeanne Champers managed our work by keeping us on target but with great sensitivity. Angie Lau, Katie Turiarcone, Rosa Casillas, and Mimi Navaro helped us in the office. These four ladies expedited the technical dimensions of our work in the most diligent and skillful ways. To these six women we extend our heartfelt thanks.

And finally, we thank each of our four grandchildren for often waiting patiently until at least one of us would take time off from the book to spend and to grow together.

Foreword

The authors, Naftaly and Lynette Glasman, have written the book that we've all been waiting for. It treats, head on, the critical issue of school accountability: who's responsible in education for whom, where, and to what ends, both personal and public.

In the larger and ideal sense, we are all responsible—if not accountable—for the upbringing of our children. After all, we pay taxes to raise the necessary $360 billion annually to educate the nearly fifty-four million school-age children in pre-K–12 public education. And under the mantle of "public" schooling, we participate in the political system that elects school board members, governors, and even the president of the United States, who help to identify (and appoint) educational leaders (such as the U.S. Secretary of Education or State Commissions of Education), who in turn certify teachers, build and maintain school buildings, and set standards and issue diplomas.

Parents too are educators—often the primary caregivers—who send their offspring to school in good faith: with the hope that children will learn to become happy, productive adults, knowledgeable voters, and active citizens in their community and society. And in schools, principals and teachers are accountable to one another as colleagues, and to parents and the community as trained professionals. So accountability is the very glue that holds schools together—the stated and unspoken norms and procedures that make schools work and improve.

The Glasmans' new book, *The Expert School Leader: Accelerating Accountability*, shows that education—and educators—are all accountable for the schooling of our children in complex and sometimes confusing ways.

First, schoolteachers and administrators are part of an increasingly demanding profession, now better paid and more highly respected than ever before. And these educators are bonded together, in what might be called professional accountability—the collective norms of being a vital service provider.

Second, educators are also influenced and controlled by direct and indirect political control, whereby schools are now regulated by federal (e.g., No Child Left Behind and the Individuals with Disabilities Education Act), state, and local regulations, standards, and tests. We might call this regulatory accountability.

Third, teachers and administrators work closely together in schools, seeking to provide a safe, healthy, and happy education to students, creating a form of cultural accountability, where the norms and expectations of the school as a social system have enormous influence on the behavior of adults and children within their walls.

It's this third form of accountability that mainly occupies the Glasmans in their new book, which is extraordinary in its breadth—comparing leaders in a wide range of jobs, such as choral conductors, hospital chaplains, automobile service advisors, and even a traffic cop—giving us a broad view of what leaders do, how they hold others accountable while being responsible professionals themselves. From these interviews, the authors extract a very useful framework for understanding the competencies that all leaders need in building better institutions and holding themselves and their colleagues accountable:

- From an airline captain, school leaders can learn about achieving predetermined goals;
- From a traffic police officer, we are aware of maintaining safety and enforcing rules;
- From a crop grower, we see the advantages of maximizing benefits that accrue to students for a given cost;
- From an automotive service advisor, we are encouraged to problem solve;
- From a chief financial officer, we see the importance of assuming fiduciary responsibilities;
- From a hospital chaplain, we realize the need to provide spiritual guidance and comfort;
- From a courtroom judge, we know about managing conflict; and
- From a choral conductor comes the importance of improving future performance based on recent efforts and results.

From in-depth interviews with each of these leaders, we learn much about what accountability means and can do for schools. Take one poignant example from chapter 8: a CFO (chief financial officer), according to the authors, reported the importance of fiscal accountability to all organizations. He stated, "In my capacity as CFO, I am intimately and completely familiar with all operational incomes except fundraising. I negotiate contracts and supervise their implementation from a financial perspective. I also control the flow of financial information" (79). The lessons for school accountability are comparable, in high relief: managing the money and the information about how these funds are raised and spent. Without these systems and insights, school leaders can hardly be accountable—great example.

Thus, the first half of the book details the nature of accountability of nine types, using noneducators as living examples, ranging from a hospital chaplain attending to the souls of the flock to a car service head whose job is moving automobiles through a system of diagnosis and repair. We learn much from both of these different supervisors and from their settings, which are different—but similar—to schools.

The second half of the book shifts to school leaders and their accountability systems, which become clearer and more engaging for the breadth of the related others. Take safety as a critical element of accountability: while air safety is vitally important to aircraft leaders and passengers, schools are also worried about the well-being of their students and the importance of students' arriving on time, being instructed by the clock, and being safe at all times. It's the connection between educational accountability and similar concerns elsewhere that gives this book its power and interest. What teachers and principals face is not an isolated concern, as this book shows over and over again.

To support their claim, the Glasmans instilled the recommendations made by the noneducators and tested their validity with close to one hundred secondary and elementary school leaders. They asked these practitioners to comment on the usefulness and feasibility of implementing these recommendations, and most were perceived as being useful. The Glasmans report numerous examples of proposed ways of implementing these ideas in the schools.

The final part of *The Expert School Leader* looks at improving school accountability, based on what we've learned from other occupations and roles in modern organizations. How can educators, and other professionals, acquire and use these special skills to make themselves and their schools more accountable? All the Glasmans' wisdom, insights, and knowledge come to bear in this last section—providing the skills to achieve goals, handle "problematic situations" (154), keep schools safe and sound for staff members and students, and help children to learn to be good citizens and able learners.

In the epilogue, the authors see their book—and our lives—as a "journey that began with considering demands for educational accountability that are placed on school leaders and ended with . . . the importance of the evaluation process to assess how accountable school leaders have become" (161). While the Glasmans acknowledge some limitations of the book, including few examples of racial and social diversity, and the missing "context of the information-technology age," we are all the wiser and stronger from this analysis. We see, as we're told, that accountability is affected by both substance and image, based on major competencies. We are all better off— yes, stronger—for having experienced this amazing book. Being wiser and more accountable can only benefit our schools, their staff, and most importantly, our children.

Bruce S. Cooper, chair and professor,
Division of Educational Leadership, Administration, and Policy,
Fordham University Graduate School of Education

I

SCHOOL LEADERS NEED SPECIAL LENSES

1

Demands for
School Accountability

As standardized test scores have exposed weaknesses in student performance, the public and its representatives (elected officials, PTA members, etc.)
have made increasing demands on school leaders to improve student
achievement. No Child Left Behind is just the most visible of recent attempts to improve student learning and make schools more accountable.

This book paints school leader accountability with a broader brush. We
view being accountable as assuming responsibility for the total operation of
a school. That includes student achievement, certainly—and very importantly! But it also includes such other things as assuring students' safety,
managing the school's finances judiciously, and solving problems of all
sorts on an ongoing basis.

All of the aspects of school functioning must be the responsibility of the
school leader. Dealing with them, then, actually constitutes the job description of that leader. Therefore, we define school leader accountability as
the degree of success that a school leader has in fulfilling his or her job requirements.

HOW CAN WE TRAIN AND PREPARE
ACCOUNTABLE SCHOOL LEADERS?

After a decade of trying to escape their share of the blame that had been focused on education, those responsible for school-leadership-preparation
programs began to seriously examine how they could help relieve the crisis.
Professional concerns for leadership-preparation accountability have given
rise to new initiatives.

For example, in 2001 the National Commission for the Enhancement of School Leadership Preparation Programs (of which the first author was a member) called for an in-depth study of the problem (e.g., Glasman 2002; Murphy and Vriesenga 2004). Various criteria were proposed for judging and improving the quality of the programs that prepare school leaders.

It did not take long for most of the stakeholders involved in the preparation programs to focus on the internship experience as the pivotal component of the programs (Davis et al. 2005; Glasman, Cibulka, and Ashby 2002). Efforts were extended to integrate acquired academic knowledge with practical preparation experiences.

The earlier suggestions about how to make the internship a more effective preparatory experience for the leadership job were incomplete (Glasman and Heck 1992/1993). There was a lacking of curricular work that should have been anchored in the assumption that the internship and the preparatory program as a whole are but the initial step in the needed ongoing process of learning over the entire career of the school leader, particularly as it relates to change (Duke 2004).

On the basis of some key literature on leadership and leadership accountability in education and related fields (e.g., Boyan 1988; Bennis and Nanus 1985; Leithwood and Duke 1999), we see accountability as the glue that binds together what leaders actually do. And we view what they do as responding to eight sets of demands, each of which creates a corresponding challenge that schools leaders must face and meet.

EIGHT SETS OF DEMANDS MADE ON SCHOOL LEADERS AND THE CORRESPONDING CHALLENGES THEY MUST FACE AND MEET

First set of demands: it is the responsibility of the school leader to guide the process of setting goals for the school early in the year and to achieve those goals by the end of the year.

Challenge 1: achieving predetermined school goals.

Second set of demands: it is the responsibility of the school leader to minimize and, if possible, eliminate misbehavior and violence (including armed violence) in the school.

Challenge 2: maintaining safety and rule enforcement in school by patrolling the school grounds.

Third set of demands: it is the responsibility of the school leader to maximize the quantity and quality of student learning within a given budget.

Challenge 3: enhancing the learning benefits that students accrue in school per given cost.

Fourth set of demands: it is the responsibility of the school leader to solve problems when possible and to not allow major problems to escalate.
Challenge 4: solving and helping to solve problems in the school.
Fifth set of demands: it is the responsibility of the school leader to learn how to manage school finances and use school money judiciously and fairly.
Challenge 5: assuming fiduciary responsibility in the school.
Sixth set of demands: it is the responsibility of the school leader to provide solace to individuals and groups in the school when tragedies occur or when punishment is required.
Challenge 6: providing emotional support when needed in the school.
Seventh set of demands: it is the responsibility of the school leader to develop and utilize methods of handling and resolving conflicts in a fair and equitable manner.
Challenge 7: managing and adjudicating conflicts in the school community.
Eighth set of demands: it is the responsibility of the school leader to improve student test scores in any way feasible and to publicize the scores annually.
Challenge 8: making beneficial uses of student achievement data for the purposes of improving performance and marketing the school's achievements.

Chapter 2 in this book describes each of the above challenges in detail. The chapter is based on the method of anecdotal inquiry that Cousins (1983) uses when he describes challenges that exist in the practice of medicine. This strategy is based on highlighting what is reported and then analyzing that information.

Numerous school-leadership interns with whom we have interacted over the last seven years have helped us select and articulate the eight challenges. As interns who were almost ready to go out into the world of school-leadership practice, they taught us a great deal from their idealistic expectations for their careers. The final list of challenges that was selected is based to a large extent on their input. We sincerely thank them.

In summary, beginning with this chapter we will describe a chain of four elements associated with school-leadership accountability. The demands for this accountability constitute the first link on this chain. The second link is the corresponding challenges faced by school leaders. Next is the corresponding competencies needed in order to face and meet these challenges—the third link. The fourth link involves a description of the time frames and ways in which these corresponding competencies can be acquired.

Before we move on to a discussion of the challenges (second link in this chain), we wish to mention a particularly uncomplimentary view of the notion of accountability as it is presented in school-leadership-preparation programs. Hess and Kelly (2005a) have reported that accountability is indeed mentioned in some preparatory programs in relation to school management by results. But in a follow-up study of texts used in these programs (Hess and Kelly 2005b), it was noted that accountability was mentioned only five times per one hundred pages of text, 20 percent in a positive fashion, 57 percent in a neutral way, and 23 percent in a negative or hostile manner. This means that accountability was mentioned in leadership-preparation texts only one time per one hundred pages in a positive manner. The authors also found that "just 2% of 2,424 course weeks address accountability" (36) and that there is "misuse of accountability instruments" (38). These authors call for paying increased attention to the important issue of accountability in school-leadership-preparation programs.

Browder (1971) and Firestone and Shipps (2005) asked for increased attention to the issue of accountability in school-leadership practice. This book is designed to do just that.

2

Challenges Leaders Face

SCHOOL GOALS

The challenge of achieving predetermined school goals is often taken for granted; at best, it is underrated. Yet year in and year out, schools are expected to enroll both returning and new students and lead them as individuals and as a school toward achieving predetermined goals. Toward this end the school is expected to provide all students with instructional and other services designed to achieve various intellectual, psychological, moral, social, and civic goals. School leaders face this challenge within a structure of governance that includes the federal government, the state government, the school district, and several other related county and local units.

Broad goals are revisited annually above the school level, particularly at the school district level. The more specific goals are revisited primarily inside the school. School districts vary in the extent to which they actually empower individual school leaders to engage in the development of predetermined goals at their school level.

On one end of the continuum, there is typically a districtwide three-to-five-year strategic plan that includes predetermined goals for all of the district's schools. In such a case, individual school leaders are expected to pursue and meet the challenge of achieving these predetermined school goals.

On the other end of the continuum, there is a broadly articulated vision for the district as a whole. Such a vision leaves each individual school leader with the authority to develop and implement specific goals for her or his school. In some such cases, teachers and even parents participate in the development of these goals. Examples might include learning to read in English for the non-English speakers, mastering of certain mathematical concepts, and learning about the local community by participating in some of its activities. Regardless of the point on this imaginary continuum of goal development for the school, the challenge of achieving those goals is the responsibility of the individual school leader. This is the case even if the predetermined goals change as a result of external and internal changes.

In their efforts to achieve predetermined goals, school leaders need to be involved with a large number of youths and adults. This kind of responsibility is a major and pivotal challenge. It is also complex and demanding. It involves unexpected developments that must be handled with knowledge, skills, and determination but also with caution.

SAFETY AND RULE ENFORCEMENT

In June 2005 a San Diego superior court jury awarded two former high school students a total of $300,000. The jury found that school administrators failed to protect these gay students from other students who harassed them because of their sexual orientation. "Students called me names," said one of the two former students, "vandalized my car, shoved me in the hallways, threw food and spit at me over a period of several years ever since I was a freshman."

The student's attorney said that the school staff had advised these students "to just brush it off, to ignore it." Following the jury's decision, the district superintendent said that the school staff had provided the students with "significant support" and that the district would probably appeal the decision. This unsafe school environment for two students featured hate, possibly unmanaged anger, bullying, damage to property, and dangerous physical contact (Sullivan, Cleary, and Sullivan 2004). It involved violence and breaking the law.

In 1997 a high school student in Pearl, Mississippi, killed two students. Five months later, four students and a teacher were murdered in a Jonesboro, Arkansas, middle school. A mere one month later, a teacher was killed at a high school in Edinboro, Pennsylvania. Two months after that, two students were murdered in a Springfield, Oregon, high school. Many people were also injured in these incidents.

The incident that probably most shocked the nation as a whole occurred in April 1999 at Columbine High School in Littleton, Colorado. Two students murdered twelve others plus a teacher and then took their own lives. Vuillemainroy (2004) reports that during the twelve months following Columbine twenty-five shooting incidents occurred in schools across the nation. This was an unparalleled set of armed violence incidents in American schools. Reportedly, what typically happens in such situations is that one or more armed students enter the school and immediately begin to shoot to kill and injure. Most of the time the shooting stops after police are summoned and subdue the perpetrators.

In the face of such tragedies, the challenge facing school leaders in maximizing safety and rule enforcement is very, very crucial. When such violence occurs, not only are lives lost and people seriously injured but also learning stops for a while, and the need for psychological support and services becomes necessary for many students and adults.

Patrolling the school grounds provides leadership presence that enhances leader accountability. Potential perpetrators of violence would become increasingly cautious as a result of such presence, so this can be viewed as a preventive measure. It also provides for dealing on the spot with observed violation of the law and unruly behavior. In meeting this challenge, school leaders will also encounter issues associated with student rights, especially when law-enforcement personnel are called onto the campus. This increases the complexity associated with meeting this challenge.

STUDENT BENEFITS

School leaders are expected to enhance the learning benefits that the school provides to all students. Each increase of benefit should be considered in relation to a given unit of cost. This kind of efficiency contributes to leader accountability. Benefits are defined as school programs, personnel, and in general, experiences that contribute to student learning. Benefits also include decreases in detentions, expulsions, and dropouts. In such cases, student-learning time increases. Student and parent satisfaction are counted as benefits, too. The key-outcome benefits include student test scores on domain-referenced and norm-referenced tests. Enhancing the benefits for a unit of costs implies improving leader accountability.

Allocating categorical funds is limited to attempts to improve learning activities for which the funds are earmarked. General funds can be earmarked for any learning activity limited only by the available amount of funding. In either case, changes in learning benefits may occur with a proportional increase of cost or without it.

When resources are added to fund certain activities, then the total benefits include those accrued from the said activities minus those forgone from not funding other activities. Thus, a choice could include adding a college preparatory class in a particular secondary school or adding a remedial reading class for incoming ninth graders in the same school. Another choice might be adding a teacher or four part-time teacher's aids to the lower grades of a particular elementary school.

The above examples involve the cost of employing additional personnel. The added cost would be relatively easy to figure out. The added benefits that are directly related to this added cost are not as easily assessed. Benefits might not be the same for every student in quantity and quality. Benefits may also be of the cognitive, emotional, social, and future job-related type. Also, there might be some factors that relate to the added benefits other than the hiring of more personnel. Quality of instruction, student ability and motivation, and the social atmosphere of the classrooms are but a few examples of such factors.

School leaders need to enhance efforts to maximize those factors that might have positive effects on the outcome benefits. Effective guidance of the additional personnel may be one example. Encouraging and motivating students in special classes is another example. At times, of course, there is a simultaneous need to minimize factors that might have negative effects on outcome benefits. Such factors should include limiting student enrollment in advanced or remedial classes.

It is possible to think of several different kinds of added benefits that school leaders might promote. The literature on educational evaluation includes many suggestions designed to improve accountability. Very little is reported about who implements these suggestions and how they do so, who pays for it, and what the effects of this implementation are. Objective assessments of effects are hampered by vested interests and by school leaders' general lack of assessment skills. Yet school leader accountability or the lack thereof has been shaped so far in significant ways by vested interests and levels of evaluation skills.

PROBLEM SOLVING

Survey after survey shows that school leaders claim to spend the majority of their time helping to solve problems. But is this valid? Perhaps, but this repeated finding implies that they perceive it that way. School leaders may view this more as a personal than a professional challenge. The argument that is often heard is as follows: "I wish I could spend more time on instruction, but there are so many problems to which I need to attend every single day."

School leaders spend a great deal of their time helping to solve other people's problems. In the school there are students, teachers, and other staff members. In and around the school one finds parents, guardians, suppliers, repair people, public officials, and other stakeholders. This is a large number of different people who may have many different problems.

The range of problems is extremely wide, and available information about them varies in relevancy, accuracy, and complexity. For example, pupils' learning problems emerge separately from or in combination with psychological, behavioral, and social problems. There are often problems associated with personnel competence or attitude. A need for a particular school-related service can pose a problem. Safety inadequacies, budgetary shortfalls, unsuitable structural configurations, and fuzzy legal boundaries are but some examples of typical problems.

Which school leader possesses all the needed expertise to provide help in solving all possible problems? To determine what a given problem actually is and what kind of help is needed to solve it is only the first step in pursuit of this type of challenge.

As they help solve problems, school leaders are involved simultaneously with a variety of people and a variety of issues. At any given time they are engaged in different phases of solutions to different problems. Leader accountability involves remembering a large amount of information about different issues and people. There is also the need to prioritize problems by degree of urgency.

School leaders might first become aware of a problem when it pops up. Or it might come to their attention long after unsuccessful attempts have been made by others to solve it. To help solve a problem accountably could take many forms, from simply helping to define the problem to offering additional resources in order to solve the problem to actually being involved in the solution. There are problems that cannot be solved, just managed. There are problems that must be solved immediately, and there are problems that must remain unattended to, at least for a while.

Actual involvement in solving all of these types of problems as well as reflecting on them to maximize effectiveness may cause the leader stress (Fullan 2005). School leaders must be able to store and recall the exact status of each problem that is at hand. Then, on the basis of what their data and gut feelings tell them, they must continuously maintain and alter priorities to deal with these problems. They must also communicate effectively about their involvement in the problem and its solution (Glasman 1994; Glasman and Crowson 1998).

FIDUCIARY RESPONSIBILITY

It is difficult for school leaders to be financially accountable in highly centralized school districts. First, education is a highly intensive labor industry, and the teachers' salary schedule is determined at the district level. Second, the authority of school leaders related to levels of incomes and nonpersonnel expenditures is limited. Third, we are in a time when the fiscal posture of many schools is not good.

In several districts, reserves are depleted to a level below what the state recommends. Some school districts even operate with a deficit. One hears of school closures, teachers being put on notice of layoff, and programs being cut, especially noncore classes such as athletics, the arts, advanced courses, and remedial programs. Yet, assuming fiduciary responsibility is a must for school leaders.

Assuming fiduciary responsibility relates to school revenues, expenditures, and school programs. Most of the school income comes from the state in the form of general aid. This aid is based on the number of students enrolled in the school district. State aid formulae are also based on a number of criteria that are related to each district's special circumstances and needs (e.g., rural circumstances, special education needs).

In addition, formulae include efforts to reduce financial inequality among districts. This is done by placing caps on the tax rate that districts can impose on their properties to generate additional money to augment the state allocations. The state and the federal government also fund special programs, typically in the form of categorical aid.

The expenditure side of the budget is laden with challenging issues. One issue is that an educational program might be mandated but without sufficient funds to cover its implementation. Recent examples include the 2002 No Child Left Behind federal legislation and the 2004 special education legislation enacted in several states. In the former case, some state and local leaders revolted as they evaluated programs by using state rather than federal criteria. Other states made questionable inter-item budgetary transfers in an attempt to abide by the law. Still others bypassed the law, thereby forfeiting the accompanying financial support altogether.

Frequently having insufficient time to plan how to spend the money within the school is a problem. If highly desired, temporary, part-time personnel cannot be hired on time, these individuals accept positions elsewhere. If programmatic choices are made too late, external funding might be lost. At times, there are not enough matching funds available that are required to apply for entitlement grants. There are even cases of corruption in some school districts, where the state has to take over the management of that district's budget as a result. In such cases, the local school leader is usually not authorized to write checks.

The assumption of fiduciary responsibility also involves the examination of programs. But often, due to certain laws related to certain programs that the school must provide, there are difficulties in minimizing financial inefficiency. Competing pressures to attend to needs of diverse students make the prioritization of educational objectives difficult due to value differences and student diversity.

Living with fiduciary responsibility in a not-for-profit organization such as a school is a tough pill to swallow. School people are not used to living within the context of financial rewards or punishments. Teachers are usually vehemently against merit pay, for example. Their professional organizations fight any attempts by state legislatures to enact a law that relates to accountability in this manner. Attempts by the executive branch to place such ideas on state ballots are always resisted by teachers' unions.

The challenge of assuming fiduciary responsibility in economic bad times implies making extremely difficult budgetary choices. Even in economic good times, human nature and politics are such that financial resources are always scarce. Competition for them is always intense. Concurrent demands for educational excellence, equality, and efficiency are always there. And there are very few school leaders whose formal training in financial management is adequate in the areas related to school finance. Ideally, to manage the budget well, a school leader should be well versed in the areas of government services and funding, accounting, law, human resources, and business management.

EMOTIONAL COMFORT

Difficult times had befallen one of the junior high schools in Santa Barbara, California. A combination of unexpected difficult situations and unwise decisions had brought about stress, pain, and hopelessness. Had school leaders been willing and able to provide emotional support and comfort, suffering would have been minimized. In fifteen years the school lost half of its students and teachers, much revenue, and its wonderful reputation. Too few people cared for the school's welfare and searched for ways to help it. And those few folks had too little authority to do anything that would halt the downward fall.

In 1992 the school was named one of the top schools in the state. But in 2005 the school was bleeding profusely and needed stronger emotional support by school leaders to minimize the rate at which students were transferring to other schools. Personnel turnover could also have been lowered. Parental anger and unnecessary personal agonies could have been minimized.

What was the source of the challenge in Santa Barbara that required providing solace to those in need? No one died or became physically ill. No one was murdered or physically injured. There were no major catastrophes such as fire, flood, or earthquake. Yet a need for emotional comfort was heard loud and clear, over and over again.

There was a need to provide social support to the drove of newcomers who were moving into the area. Slow learners needed academic and psychological support. Disappointed and discouraged teachers needed a boost to their pride and motivation. Uninformed parents and guardians needed to develop hope. High-performing students and their parents needed guarantees that excellence would continue to exist. Had these types of support offers been made, there would probably have not been a serious increase in the leaders' demands for accountability in this school.

But few of these attempts were made. Student enrollment in adjacent elementary schools had increased due to a rapid influx into the area of low-income immigrant Latino families. The district's board of education decided to move sixth-grade classes from primarily poorer scoring elementary schools to this junior high school. No other junior high school in the district was dealt with this way even though student populations were growing in all of the elementary schools throughout the district.

Leaders in this junior high school remained silent. Soon sixth graders entered this junior high school. No additional services were provided for them. No pre–junior high school needs were met. The number of teachers in the school grew but not enough to handle the demand. Space filled up and then became overcrowded. Very little emotional support was to be found in the early years of this new structure of a sixth-through-eighth-grade school. With time, the need for support and comfort intensified because things became worse. Most sixth graders were in academic and social trouble. Detention increased. School attendance dropped. The district's continuation high school enrolled more and more of this school's graduates.

No one provided emotional support of any kind to the students, teachers, staff members, and parents. By 1999, one-third of the former teachers had left. An increasing number of parents moved their children to other junior high schools in the district. The student population in the school dropped by one-half. As a result, revenues were lost. The proportion of slow learners rose significantly. The school turned from having an excellent reputation to being viewed as extremely problematic.

Instead of beginning to provide some emotional support before things got even worse, the school leadership decided to portray a desperate school that needed more money. Then, a huge mistake was made. The leadership posted test results of students in the hall of the school, including a breakdown of the results by race and ethnicity. The principal claimed that he posted these results in this way in order to convince the district's administration that the need for funding for Latino students was great.

This tactic backfired. Latino students and their parents became highly embarrassed. Controversy erupted in the school regarding the extent to which needs of Latino students were being met. The school leadership provided no support and no hope for any of the families. No one explained to non-English (or even to English-speaking) parents what the test results meant. No one pointed out, for example, that some Latino students were doing better than in the past year. Also, no one pointed out to those Anglo parents whose children were still attending the school that their children were doing as well as their counterparts in the district's other junior high schools.

Even more Anglo students were now taken out of this school by their parents and transferred to other junior high schools in the district. More teachers left. There were additional budget cuts made due to decreased enrollment. Some special curricula were eliminated. Still, no emotional support was offered to either those who departed or to those who remained at the school.

Fast-forwarding three school leaders later, some remaining teachers and families who had provided solace to each other decided to place demands on the district administration. Their request was for the district to temporarily take upon itself the role of leading the school into a new era of trust and renewal. But even at that level of administration (i.e., central office control), no one offered emotional support.

In an arbitrary way, the district administration decided that, since there was no consensus among the parties in the school as to how the school should proceed, a set of mediators needed to be hired (at great financial expense). New temporary leadership was installed. Still, no attempt was made to heal the open wounds.

In 2002 the acting principal told us that his leadership role was to be a two-to-three-year rejuvenator. Parents intimated to us that without a sense of hope, more of them would be removing their children from the school and enrolling them elsewhere. The principal left before the end of the first year of service.

At the end of the 2003–2004 school year, a retired principal was hired as a leader to again try to rejuvenate the school. We found her to be an impressive leader, engaging in lots of interpersonal relationships and emphasizing academic learning. But she was not a healer. Nothing changed in the school, and she resigned fourteen months later. A focus on providing emotional comfort and support to everyone in the school was clearly lacking. To pursue this kind of a challenge, as this case shows, is difficult. The district leadership did not provide help. There was no expression of sensitivity or empathy made toward the entire population of this junior high school.

CONFLICT RESOLUTION

Conflicts emerge when two or more sides cannot resolve opposing desires to do something or cannot solve disagreements among themselves. If conflicts remain unresolved, managing them is a major challenge where the attempt is to avoid unwanted battles and even tragic consequences.

In the context of diminishing resources, for example, a conflict may arise over not wanting to cut any performing arts classes and not wanting to raise class size in other elective courses. Since parents want what they think is best for their children, this conflict would be between the parents of the performing arts students and other students' parents. Likewise, a conflict may arise between parents or teachers who feel that not enough personnel are hired as precautionary measures to violence and others who feel that not enough personnel are hired for remedial instruction.

School leaders who worry about being accountable in terms of not leaving such conflicts unresolved need to set the stage for an orderly and fair articulation of the positions. Next, they have to attempt to resolve the conflict by making relevant decisions, explaining them, and even offering additional alternatives. During this process, school leaders at times will have to deal with lack of satisfaction on the part of some individuals involved in the conflict, emotional outbursts, antagonism, appeals to higher authorities, and even threats of different sorts.

The tough conflicts that school leaders find hard to resolve are conflicts that they will end up having to manage but with insufficient authority to do so. For example, decisions made by higher governmental authorities to which the schools must respond but cannot do so easily may create a myriad of conflicts—among teachers, between teachers and parents, or between the school leader and the district administration.

The 2002 No Child Left Behind federal legislation that was mentioned earlier, for example, called for measuring school progress in certain ways from year to year. The legislation also included a total allocation of twenty-five billion dollars awarding twenty-five thousand dollars annually to each school whose progress was considered successful according to the mandated measures. The House of Representatives voted 381 to 41 in favor of this legislation. In the Senate the vote was 87 to 10.

It soon became apparent that, based on the federal measurement guidelines, many schools were scoring poorly. Teachers and parents were disappointed. Many people became angry and called the legislation inappropriate. School leaders had to deal with a conflict between what the federal government mandated and what key people in their schools believed. The worst conflicts among some school people were created as a result of an external mandate over which they had no authority.

Democrats in Washington began to find fault with the implementation of the legislation. State and educational officials wrote to Washington asking for adjustments in the ways student achievement should be measured. Teachers' unions instructed their members to express opposition to the perceived intent of the federal government to use low scores on the mandated tests as reasons for not providing additional funding to schools. Unions stated that schools were indeed making progress but that the mandated tools to measure this progress were inappropriate.

School leaders found themselves engaged in efforts to manage conflicts whose outcomes they could not control and therefore did not have any chance of resolving. The only thing most leaders could do and did do was to keep encouraging teachers to continue what they were doing (and doing well).

During 2003 these conflicts intensified and became widespread. In several school districts the mandated measures showed no improvement in scores. In other districts, scores actually plummeted. Many local school leaders argued that these tests did not measure what the students were learning.

In some states, school leaders urged their districts and their state leadership to secure help from educational researchers whose expertise is measuring student achievement. They were hoping for changes in the methods with which student progress would be measured. Teachers rejected some of the proposed changes. There were school leaders who wanted to stop cooperating with the federal government on implementing this legislation altogether. During 2005, Connecticut, for example, continued to strongly oppose the federal mandate and would not compromise, even refusing the accompanying federal funds.

In 2005 California was one of a few states that decided to negotiate some compromises with the federal government. Its goal was to be able to use its own system of measuring school progress alongside the use of what the federal government mandated. Hundreds of schools escaped federal financial punishment as a result of these successful negotiations. Because of very strong pressure exerted by school leaders throughout the state, California actually was able to maintain its academic performance index (API) as a measuring tool.

This tool is based on the Stanford 9 test and on the California standards test in English language arts. In the California case, performance was tied directly to the state standards. Schools were ranked in comparison with other schools in the state with similar socioeconomic and ethnic characteristics (called bands). Also taken into consideration were the percentages of students with limited English skills, the parent education levels, and the percentage of teachers in the school who possessed an emergency teaching credential instead of full accreditation.

Despite the adjustments, the annual California API state reports in 2005 were still discouraging. Many schools scored quite poorly. The disappointment and anger in some of these schools was intense, particularly in low socioeconomic schools that had progressed quite significantly but, according to the federal way of measuring progress, had not progressed sufficiently to qualify for federal funds. School leaders experienced difficulties in explaining to the school stakeholders what was happening. On their part, state officials were satisfied that the state was in compliance with federal requirements.

School leaders even had to get involved in the methods used to score the test questions. The demand for accountability forced them to get involved. School leaders could not resolve conflicts in this area; they only managed the situation in several different ways. Some acted surprised; they pretended not to understand why the scores were low. They did so because they believed that they might be viewed as being personally responsible for the scores.

Other school leaders called for rescoring the tests. Still others blamed their special education students for bringing down the average scores. A few high school leaders attributed the low scores to changes in the curriculum that had been instituted on the advice of university experts. With regard to physics, for example, these school leaders suggested doing away with the changes that in their opinion amounted to diluting the curriculum and lowering expectations. There were many complaints that the tests were not sufficiently matched to what was taught. This tack amounted to blaming those who had constructed the tests.

Still other school leaders called for and organized discussions among professionals (open to the public) about what the scores actually meant, what the sources of the scores are, and what might be the right things to do about the scores. Some principals told us that they were not actually doing much, just hoping that the atmosphere would calm down with time as attention to the bad news waned. In complete contrast, others told us that they were stepping up to the plate and expressing their own opinions on what ought to be done.

USE OF ACHIEVEMENT DATA

The core issue embodied in the eighth and last challenge relates to the example described above: what should be done with the student achievement test scores? Accountable school leaders would ask more specifically, how can these scores be used to be of benefit to the students and to all stakeholders of the school? This is truly a pivotal challenge.

It is only natural that different scores would trigger different reactions from a given set of stakeholders. Relatively high scores might draw reactions of satisfaction or jealousy. Average scores may bring about happy reactions, complacency, or complaints. Relatively low scores might trigger strong resentments and complaints.

How can the conversation be focused on the beneficial uses regardless of the scores? What can be done with scores in general and with specific scores that would be helpful in improving and promoting student achievement? School-leadership accountability depends heavily on answers to these questions.

For example, what could be done with scores in order to improve instruction, and what would such actions imply about school leader accountability? Would detecting poor scores and suggesting to teachers ways of improving them increase accountability? It may sound good in theory, but pursuing the challenge of making beneficial uses of scores to improve instruction is a challenge that requires much thought and effort (Glasman and Nevo 1988). It raises at least the following questions:

Who is qualified to determine what are "poor scores"?
Are there sufficient resources to employ a professional evaluator? If not, what else should be done?
When should intervention with teachers be done?
How should teachers be involved in this work?
Who should monitor the instructional modifications, when and how?
Who examines subsequent scores, when and how?

Using student achievement information with teachers may affect instruction directly. But teachers instruct in their own ways once the classroom doors are shut. Yet school leaders are called upon to demonstrate accountability. They have to inform other stakeholders about the scores and about what is being done with them. School leaders serve as the reference point in regard to the scores for parents, community leaders, employers, and the media. Stakeholders will want to know what the scores are and what they mean. Efforts will need to be extended toward interpreting the achievement data, recognizing successes, and encouraging improvement when needed.

No matter how well students score on achievement tests parents find it difficult to accept scores if they do not feel at least partial ownership of them. Some parents do not accept the assumption that it is also their responsibility to improve student achievement. After all, they do not serve as the schoolteachers. To ask the teachers to help convince the parents to become part owners might backfire at times. Teachers themselves resist being viewed as part owners if their students do not do very well. A typical argument one hears is as follows: "I, the teacher, have no say in the selection of who I am assigned to teach and often also what I must teach; therefore, how can I be part owner of the outcome?"

To ask school district officials to help expand their own sense of ownership of the district's achievement scores could be useful, probably when the achievement scores are not too low. When they are low, then some superintendents, assistant superintendents in charge of curriculum, and personnel directors have been heard to say in private that the scores are the responsibility of the school leader who is close to the scene, not the district office.

How can we impact the development of a sense of part ownership of student scores? It involves accepting responsibility for enhancing these measures while knowing full well that formal authority regarding decisions made about what the school should do is vested in the hands of the school staff as well as the school leader. One central issue for school leaders is how to mitigate their inability to accept a request by a potential part owner who has a clear, personal vested interest in having something done in school while allowing this person to maintain a sense of ownership of the results.

Coordinating the fulfillment of various needs is a cumbersome process and also very costly in terms of people's time. This challenge might also become somewhat risky. Disagreements among part owners might lead to the development of serious conflicts. Enlisting a wider number of stakeholders in having this sense of responsibility is an important dimension of this eighth and particularly difficult challenge facing school leaders.

3

Special Competencies Leaders Need

So far it has been shown that demands for educational accountability may present themselves as eight pivotal challenges for school leaders to face and meet. This chapter shows that, in order to face and meet each challenge, school leaders need to acquire and use corresponding specialized competencies. The chapter identifies a selection of professionals who face and meet comparable challenges and who, therefore, possess core corresponding specialized competencies and use them to do their jobs.

AIRLINE CAPTAINS AND SCHOOL LEADERS BOTH NEED TO ACHIEVE PREDETERMINED GOALS

Airline captains are in command of flying planes full of passengers (or cargo) to a predetermined destination. Passengers buy tickets for the journey, board the plane, and assume that they are in the good hands of the captain and her or his crew until they arrive at their predetermined destination, where they deplane. Passengers are informed about the progress that is being made toward the arrival to these predetermined destinations. If we view schools as planes and school goals as airport destinations, then to an extent students (and their parents) should feel that they are in the good hands of the school leader and the rest of the school staff. Also to an extent, they are made aware of the progress made toward the achievement of school goals.

Most air travelers also know that the cockpit crew is guided by flight regulations and control towers and that the airline captains abide by these regulations and instructions given from the control towers. Likewise, schools have laws, mandates, policies, and regulations that guide school leaders toward the achievement of the predetermined school goals.

Airline captains are specialists in commanding an aircraft that flies with a crew and passengers toward a predetermined destination. Not infrequently, the planes have problems or the airports cannot be used at that time for taking off or landing. Transporting passengers is their primary challenge, and they face it, pursue it, and meet it daily and often several times a day. Airline captains pursue this challenge within rapidly changing organizations. On each flight they have a different crew and different passengers. They also work with different ground crews and different control towers. They do not select the members of any of these groups.

All who are involved in these organizations including the leaders and those who serve as their subordinates have very little time to get to know each other (Glasman and DelVecchio 2004, chapter 4). Followers trust leaders because leaders have been empowered to fly the plane. They trust the profession to which they belong.

In schools, only a relatively small part of the staff and the students change and that usually occurs only annually. The district staff changes infrequently, too. The relative stability of the school staff might make it easier for the school leader to depend on it in helping to pursue the challenge of achieving predetermined school goals. But the fact that school goals are less clear than airport destinations, and of the overwhelming dependence on the teachers in the achievement of the goals, necessitates specialized leadership competencies.

Another leader-staff phenomenon related to achieving goals occurs in school. Some principals have a strong say in selecting staff members for the school, for a particular grade level and for a particular class (in elementary schools and in junior high schools). This level of control might enhance the leader's effectiveness in the pursuit of school goals. But on the other hand, a number of teachers may view with a critical eye some ideas the leader has or decisions the leader makes. These teachers are in the classroom. Some of them told us that they are not sure what competencies a leader might have in pursuing goals that they (the teachers) lack.

Specialized competencies are also needed when students or their parents are not fully aware of the goals of the school and of the progress that is made toward achieving these goals. At times, such lack of awareness gives rise to uncertainties involving the reasons for this lack of information and about who should be responsible for informing them. The principal might then become concerned with issues of authority and self-confidence.

Our decision to interview an airline captain had to do with the following desires:

- to learn what being accountable means to him or her;
- to find out what the challenge of achieving predetermined destinations means;
- to become aware of what the captain actually does;
- to hear what the captain says about how she or he improves these competencies; and
- to see if the captain could offer any recommendations to school leaders on how to effectively face and meet the challenge of achieving predetermined school goals to improve their accountability.

Despite the differences between the two professions, we risked choosing an airline pilot for an interview because of the following similar criteria for accountability that are associated with this comparable challenge:

- Predetermined goals are beyond the control of both professionals.
- Client satisfaction is central with regard to process and outcome.
- Movement characterizes the process.
- And extra efforts need to be made at the start and at the end of the process.

TRAFFIC POLICE OFFICERS AND SCHOOL LEADERS BOTH NEED TO MAINTAIN SAFETY AND ENFORCE RULES (LAWS)

Traffic police officers maintain safety and enforce the law on the roads. They are professionally certified individuals who are empowered to implement these tasks. They spend most of their working hours attempting to meet this challenge. They are experts in what they are doing. They possess and use specialized competencies. The second challenge that school leaders face is maintaining safety and rule enforcement in school. To that end, they patrol the school grounds and are physically visible in other ways. But they do not spend all of their time doing that.

Traffic police officers watch and, when necessary, stop drivers who are unknown to them on the roads and highways. They typically deal with people only once. School leaders deal with students who are known to them. They get to know them even better at times when those students get in trouble more than once. School leaders deal with those who bully, use violence, carry out armed violence, and break school rules or the law with inappropriate behavior within the school grounds.

In most cases school leaders are insufficiently trained to deal with violence, especially if it comes as a dangerous surprise or is approaching a state of being out of control. Results of violent behavior may include fear, cessation of learning, injuries, damage to property, and even death. In such cases school leaders call law-enforcement personnel for help. When these kinds of things happen, the challenge of maintaining safety and enforcing the rules is absolutely critical, and demands for school leader accountability is the strongest.

We wanted to interview a traffic police officer for the purposes of discovering

- what accountability means to him;
- how he views the challenge of maintaining safety and enforcing rules;
- what he actually does;
- what views he has about how to improve these competencies; and
- what recommendations he might have for school leaders in their pursuit of the challenge of maintaining safety and enforcing rules to improve their accountability.

Despite the differences between the two professions we risked choosing a traffic police officer for an interview because of the following similar criteria in relation to the comparable challenge:

- Number, type, and consequences of inappropriate behavior are central with regard to outcome.
- Actions related to prevention characterize the process.
- And personal visibility, thoughts, actions, and sensitivities characterize the process.

CROP GROWERS AND SCHOOL LEADERS BOTH NEED TO ENHANCE BENEFITS FOR A GIVEN COST

Pursuing the third challenge of enhancing students' benefits for a given cost involves maintaining a balance between counteracting forces. One force is made up of leaders' attempts to maximize the quantity and quality of what the students experience and learn in school. Below are some examples of this:

- more effective learning-how-to-read instruction;
- a deeper understanding of society's inherent values;
- better preparation for the learning of algebra principles;
- more meaningful hands-on curriculum;
- better student appreciation of the value of good literature;
- improved accommodations of instructional programs and facilities for physically and mentally limited students;

- more college preparatory classes; and
- more job-related classes.

The counterforce is cost. School leaders should count costs as givens (sources, sizes, and fund categorizations). The challenge is to maximize benefits using the resources available. This applies to correcting learning deficiencies or trying to upgrade the performance of more capable (gifted) students. Examples might include the following:

- In teaching eighty slow beginning readers, provide part-time aids for four classrooms at the same cost of a fifth teacher because that is what the four fifth-grade teachers prefer (and there is no additional classroom space available anyway).
- And in dealing with disagreements among two sixth-grade teachers and two seventh-grade teachers regarding the desired level of understanding scientific concepts at the end of the sixth grade, develop two different internally sequenced sixth through seventh instructional programs.

We chose to interview a professional who works in both manufacturing and services. Schools produce knowledgeable and skilled students. Schools also serve students while they are in school. We identified crop growing because growers produce crops and also attend to the growth process.

There are obviously differences between teaching students and growing crops. Growers grow crops for sale and profit. Schools do not engage in sales and profit making. But both crop growers and school leaders consider the outcomes that they produce as central to their efforts. For this reason, both professionals engage in important preparatory work, long and intensive implementation work, and evaluation of the quality of products that they have produced. The criterion for measuring accountability is, thus, the same.

Crop growers prepare the ground for the seeds. They develop and construct systems within which growth is enhanced. Growers use specialists when certain problems occur that need special treatment. For school leaders, "seeds" are the students when they first come to school. The "ground" is the school itself. The "systems" are teachers, curricula, textbooks, laboratories, athletic fields, art rooms, and equipment and other materials. A need for "special treatment" may involve attending to learning and teaching problems. "Specialists" are psychologists, curriculum specialists, and others.

But clearly plants are not people. The ground in which plants grow is less complex than a school. Plants have no cognitive, motivational, affective, or psychomotor abilities. Plants have no obvious sense organs. The grower knows much more about the plant and how to grow it than anyone knows about how to produce a perfect school graduate. Losing one plant in the field is much less of a tragedy than losing a student to dropping out, expulsion, or otherwise.

Yet when difficulties in growth occur, the questions that crop growers and school leaders ask are similar:

- Which part of the growth is interfered with?
- What is (are) the cause(s) for the interference in the growth process?
- What are the costs associated with the growth process?
- And what can be done to maximize the growth process for a given cost?

It is because of evaluation criteria such as the above that are common to both professionals that we risked interviewing a crop grower. We did so despite the differences between them and school leaders. We wanted to learn about his accountability, the challenge of enhancing benefits at a given unit of cost, what he actually does, what specialized competencies he has and uses, and how he improves those competencies. We also sought recommendations he might offer about how school leaders could improve their ability to challenge and enhance student benefits at a given cost in order to improve their accountability.

AUTOMOBILE SERVICE ADVISORS AND SCHOOL LEADERS BOTH NEED TO SOLVE PROBLEMS

The fourth challenge that school leaders face is to help solve problems (typically, for a person with a problem in school). Automobile service advisors face and meet a somewhat similar challenge all day long every day. A car that comes to the auto shop with a problem (repair or service need) comes with a human being. It is a human problem as well. Right from the start we wanted to interview an automobile service advisor as our specialist in this area.

School leaders help solve problems that students, teachers, other staff members, and parents have. The school leader helps solve pedagogic and administrative problems. The automobile service advisor helps solve technical and managerial problems.

Two types of criteria relate to evaluating accountability of both the service advisor and the school leader as they solve problems. One type is associated with outcome accountability. The other is associated with process accountability. Outcome means correcting the problem or arranging for some other satisfactory solution. Process means interacting professionally and humanely with the person who has the problem.

Whether in need of service that is recommended after so many miles or in need of having a problem taken care of, a vehicle owner comes to the service department of a dealership or contacts the automobile service advisor for an appointment. The advisor listens to the driver's request or description of the problem. Following a preliminary examination the advisor suggests what should be done, checks the estimated cost of the service, has the customer sign for the work to be done, and informs the customer when the vehicle can be picked up. Detecting and arranging the solving of technical problems to the satisfaction of the customer are key components of helping repair the car's problems.

School leaders are also contacted for help in solving problems. Like the automobile service advisors, they also help identify the problems and their causes as well as what might be done, by whom, when, and with what prerequisites. Many different types of problems may arise. A relevant question becomes, what exactly are the competencies that either the service advisor or the school leader have and use in the pursuit of solving problems? This question is relevant because neither the automobile service advisor nor the school leader has a great deal of (respectively) technical or pedagogical authority over the people who actually solve the problems.

Elementary school leaders may provide some pedagogical advice to teachers. Secondary school principals are not necessarily experts in what has to be done in a particular class in a particular subject matter. The service advisor does not possess the expertise to direct the mechanic's work.

Another important difference is that school leaders have formal authority over students, and service advisors have no such authority over customers. As to teachers, the school leader has somewhat less authority over them than over students. Regarding parents, the school leader has as little authority as the advisor has over customers. Both the parent and the customer can go elsewhere if they choose.

To point out again, the decision to interview an automobile service advisor was made despite the differences between the two professions. For, there are two common criteria for evaluating these professionals for accountability: the outcome (solution) criterion and the process (interaction) criterion.

We were hoping to learn from the automobile service advisor

- how he views accountability;
- how he views the challenge of problem solving;
- what he actually does;
- what specialized competencies he has;
- how he attempts to improve those competencies; and
- what recommendations he can offer to school leaders to assist them in meeting the challenge of problem solving and becoming more accountable as a result.

CHIEF FINANCIAL OFFICERS AND SCHOOL LEADERS BOTH NEED TO ASSUME FIDUCIARY RESPONSIBILITY

Schools as nonprofit organizations receive both general and categorical (earmarked) funding. The discretion that school leaders have in relation to what they may spend is therefore unrestricted or restricted, respectively. Other nonprofit organizations are in the same situation of receiving general and categorical funding. School leaders serve as chief financial officers in their schools. In this capacity they must continuously pursue the challenge of assuming the responsibility for fiduciary matters in the school even though their finances are closely coordinated with school district officials. Chief financial officers (CFOs) in nonprofit organizations act together with chief executive officers (CEOs) in a similar way.

In our search for a nonprofit organization from which to learn about the competencies of a CFO, we looked for the kind of organization in which the CFO's fiduciary responsibility is similar to that of the school leader's. We could not find what we wanted in foundations. In several of them, lawyers work with the bank officers who manage trusts. We could not find the kind of a CFO we were looking for in any organization whose expenditure is not permitted to exceed what tax regulations require (percent of the principal and earmarked expenditures).

Our search continued in public nonprofit organizations, but in most of those that we examined, we found that the size of the core budget was too small in comparison to amounts of categorical grant monies that are raised externally. We also found that in small units one full-time or part-time accountant is employed without having a CFO, and in large units CFOs were serving as line officers heading a department with subordinates rather than as staff officers who advise the organization's CEO. None of these situations matched that of a school.

We then decided to use an additional set of related criteria in our search. We looked for a nonprofit organization that provides services to people. The organization had to be labor intensive, and the salaries had to be determined by some schedules not under the control of the CEO. Our rationale was that such an organization would resemble the school in the following ways:

- The CEO (school leader) must assume fiduciary responsibilities despite the fact that she or he controls only a very small percentage of the size and nature of the income (state, federal, and school district sources) and a very small percentage of the size and nature of the expenditures (discretionary expenditures within the school).
- The minimal control of income and expenditure would be our key criterion for selection because of the difficulties associated with assuming fiduciary responsibilities under such conditions.

- This kind of demand for leadership accountability is not only a fiduciary challenge but a moral one, too: being responsible for resources and their use over which one has very little control (formal authority).

We found a CFO who is employed in a nonprofit organization that serves people, a rehabilitation institute. The institute must follow certain laws. It is labor intensive. The professionals who are employed there are compensated on the basis of a salary schedule, and some of them also have individual contracts. The CFO is the person who is fiscally accountable for the institute. The reports that he submits deal with accountability associated with the entire institute despite the existence of a salary schedule for most of the professionals working there. We interviewed the CFO with the hope that awareness about some of the specialized competencies that he has acquired and uses would be beneficial to school leaders.

HOSPITAL CHAPLAINS AND SCHOOL LEADERS BOTH NEED TO PROVIDE COMFORT WHEN NEEDED

Providing comfort when needed in school is the sixth challenge we have identified that school leaders face. Who else might provide comfort and emotional support to individuals within an organizational context? In which organizations is such comfort most frequently needed and professionally done? What kind of a professional might be pursuing this kind of challenge on a regular and frequent basis? Awareness of which specialized competencies that enhance the pursuit of providing comfort might school leaders benefit from? The use of which of those competencies would improve the leaders' accountability?

The immediate thought was of hospital chaplains. Their days are filled with providing comfort to different individuals: the ill, the injured, the dying, and their loved ones. Clergy who are employed in houses of prayer visit their parishioners when they are hospitalized. They provide them with comfort. But hospitals that employ their own members of the clergy expect them to provide spiritual care to the entire hospital's patients and staff members. Spiritual caregivers provide opportunities for patients and their dear ones to share freely whatever emotions they experience.

In schools, there are several times when students, their peers, their parents, and teachers would need emotional support. There is ridicule. There is theft. There is violence, at times, armed violence. There is bodily harm, at times, serious and even fatal injuries. There may be a natural disaster on the campus or awareness of one elsewhere. And then there are punishments that include detentions, suspensions, and expulsions. There is retention at grade level. There is transfer and also dropout.

Emotional support is needed. It is a major challenge to provide strong emotional support. The delivery (process) has to be of high quality. School leaders often cannot do it all. Other staff members need to join in the pursuit of this challenge. They and not only the school leader must possess related specialized competencies. Staff members must be trained to help pursue this challenge. We interviewed a hospital chaplain in order to learn about what these professionals do, their specialized competencies, how they improve upon them, what exactly is emotional support, how one becomes accountable in this field, and what recommendations could be made about how school leaders can improve their pursuit of this challenge.

COURTROOM JUDGES AND SCHOOL LEADERS BOTH NEED TO MANAGE CONFLICT

The seventh challenge that we believe school leaders must pursue includes the process of managing and adjudicating conflicts in schools. Courtroom judges pursue a comparable challenge. Indeed, they are specialists in pursuing such a challenge. They possess and use specialized competencies, including knowledge, skills, and aptitude. This challenge is the heart of their work.

Contentious situations are brought before the court. The considerations used by the judge in court are primarily legal in nature. In schools, contentious situations may or may not involve legal considerations. But there are significant similarities between the two sets of conditions.

Conflicts that both the courtroom judge and the school leader face are unsettled differences between two parties. That is why there is a conflict. In a civil case, when the judge is unsuccessful in having the two parties settle their differences out of court, the case goes to court. The judge then presides over the court proceedings until a judgment is made with regard to the case. In school, too, efforts are first made to work things out informally. If unsuccessful, the school leader needs to initiate a more comprehensive and orderly factfinding process with both parties being aware of the process. Both in court and in school the process has to be managed in a professional manner.

Yet clearly a school is not a court of law. Pedagogic or administrative theories might guide the behavior of the school leader in dealing with conflicts, but these theories are insufficiently precise and insufficiently reliable. By contrast, even laws that are ambiguous are considered precise and reliable guides to taking legal actions. That is the chief reason the process of handling conflicts in schools is not as carefully spelled out as are court proceedings, even if the judge at times uses her or his subjective discretion about procedures.

In addition, the school leader cannot easily obtain tools with which to examine the credibility of information that involved individuals provide. The judge has better tools that are more concrete. Another factor that might determine the behavior of the manager/adjudicator of a conflict is the following: Once a conflict is over the judge will not see those involved in the conflict again. The school leader must continue to interact with these people.

Therefore, it was risky to interview a courtroom judge in order to learn

- what she does;
- how she manages and adjudicates a conflict;
- what specialized competencies she has and how she improves them;
- what accountability means for her; and
- what recommendations she has for school principals for improving their own ability to manage and adjudicate conflicts in their schools.

Despite the risk, the judge has competencies that might be extremely valuable to school leaders in managing and adjudicating conflicts. In a jury trial, the judge also educates a jury and possibly others present in court. Taking on the role of education within such a context might have short- and long-term positive effects in the school.

CHORAL CONDUCTORS AND SCHOOL LEADERS BOTH NEED TO MAKE USE OF RECENT PERFORMANCE IN ORDER TO IMPROVE FUTURE PERFORMANCE

We come now to our eighth and last identified challenge that school leaders face. This challenge involves making beneficial uses of information about student achievement. Choral conductors who perform with their choruses actually engage in such tasks continuously. Their profession, almost by definition, involves extending major efforts in this direction. First they look forward to having the singers do the best that they can in the performances themselves. We really do not know all the methods that school principals employ to do the best that they can with regard to student achievement scores. Choral conductors typically engage in some key activities that occur after each performance.

First, they praise the singers, the accompanists, and all the others who have been involved with the concerts and preparation for the concerts. They do so publicly and privately. They also praise people who helped the singers personally and professionally. Choral conductors pursue such activities with specialized attitudinal and communication competencies. It is worth checking what choral conductors feel about how valuable such competencies might be for the pursuit of the comparable challenge facing school leaders with regard to student achievement, even though they do not work directly with the students. School leaders also have many more students to worry about!

Additionally, choral conductors attempt to improve the quality of future performances. Together with the singers they diagnose the performances and search for elements that might be improved. They use the "data" to guide improvement. We know of school leaders who extend major efforts to engage in the same activities, using student test scores and conferences with teachers. Test results may be useful for improvement of learning.

Choral conductors use their diagnostic/evaluative and instructional leadership competencies to pursue improvement. In so many ways, then, choral conductors and school leaders really serve as instructional leaders, too. Accountability in this area, however, would have to be measured differently because the choral conductor works with the performers, and the school leader will work with the teachers of the students.

The differences go further. Choral conductors work directly with singers prior to, during, and following concerts. Even teachers who work directly with students prior to and following the tests do not work with students during the tests. Also, singers sing as a group in a performance (there are solos, too, of course). When they take the tests, students work with no one but themselves. A related third difference is that singers may be chosen by audition to join the performing chorus. Selection of singers is the option of the choral conductor. Test taking is not optional. Choruses also work with their own budgets.

Among the differences, there is one additional key difference that might be capitalized on by school leaders if they have the competencies to pursue the challenge. The difference is in the essence of the actual achievement. The product of what the chorus performs is a collective, integrative set of sounds produced concurrently by individual singers but heard as a group sound. In school testing, the product is made up of individual student scores and even individual scores on different test items by individual students. Such scores may be summed up and talked about in numerous different ways and communicated to numerous different audiences who have a stake in the scores.

Despite the differences, we risked interviewing a choral conductor. Demands for educational accountability have increasingly focused on student achievement, a central criterion of success but lacking direct control by school leaders. The main question is what can be done with student achievement data that might give leaders some direct control over student achievement.

Choral conductors have acquired specialized competencies whose use could provide ideas to school leaders. At the least, choral conductors could talk about their specialized competencies, what they do with them, and how they strive to improve them. Perhaps if choral conductors understood the eighth challenge that school leaders face (making beneficial uses of test scores), the conductors might have some recommendations for school leaders to consider. With luck, it might be possible to learn different but useful ways of measuring accountability in this regard.

II

INTERVIEWING SPECIALISTS

4

Airline Captain Navigates toward a Predetermined Destination

"Good morning, Captain," I began. "Thanks in advance for the time. As you recall from our chat on the phone, my general interests are in what you actually do, what competencies you have to acquire and have in order to do what you do, and then also my 'dessert.' I noted the specific challenge school leaders face: achieving predetermined school goals, similar to your predetermined destinations. Hopefully you would be willing to offer some recommendations to school leaders in this regard."

Three hours later, this fifty-year-old captain was still responding extremely clearly to every question. He intimated that he had first become aware of the clarity of his mind when he began flying at age seventeen. His physics degree in college and his Air Force Undergraduate Pilot Training program (where he received his military wings) helped him, as he said, to "fully understand that to continue to improve this clarity of mind he needed to improve his knowledge and skills in flying."

He continued to be mindful of the need to remain a clear thinker during his service as a navigator for thirty months and as a pilot for seven and a half years, including three and a half years as a flight instructor. My interviewee has been flying a large American commercial aircraft since 1987. He was promoted to captain in 2004.

EXPERIENCE AND CONTROL OF WORKING SCHEDULE

"Why did you become a captain in 2004?" I asked. "Starting with something personal, hey? Just kidding," he replied. He talked about experience and seniority as qualifications. Seniority, apparently, is the key factor that determines the degree to which copilots and captains control their working schedule. Seniority also determines career advancement for copilots and the captains. I asked him to elaborate about his working schedule.

Captain: In this company competencies, qualifications, and seniority are closely related to working schedules. This relation could be better understood if personal choices that the pilot has enter into the equation. You may move up along five types of aircraft. Every captain has to have served as a copilot first. I suppose like a school principal and an assistant principal.

Author: Not always, I said.

Captain: Well they should. How could it be otherwise? How can you become responsible for a school if you have not been sitting for a while next to a person that is?

Author: I understand that your company has a seniority system.

Captain: Yes. Starting with a copilot of a Boeing 737 plane, for example, a copilot may move up through several planes to being a copilot of a Boeing 777. As some copilots gain seniority, either by the retirement of more senior pilots or by the addition of pilots because of airline expansion, some will eventually have enough seniority to hold captain positions.

Author: How are captains and pilots chosen for particular aircraft?

Captain: In my company, particular planes are chosen for particular flights. Then, captains and copilots are assigned to the planes.

Author: So captains do not choose their copilots.

Captain: No, they do not.

Author: Do you consider your copilot part of your "administration"?

Captain: Only for any given flight. This applies to the rest of the crew as well. The passengers, too.

Author: How does it feel, Captain? If I led a school today, and somebody assigned a number 2 person to me—and a crew and passengers—every day or week, I do not know if I could handle that. It reminds me of a summer camp director who has different counselors and different kids every week. Are you comfortable with such arrangements? You have to be, I suppose.

Captain: Yes, that is the nature of our job. You face the same challenge anew on every flight. Each time it is up to you to reach the destination. And that is how you gain experience, too.

Author: You are a new captain, if I may say so, sir. Are you happy with where you are right now?

Captain: I am extremely happy where I am right now. It is where I want to be.

Author: What do you mean by "where"?

Captain: I mean at my job and salary level. Movement to a larger aircraft implies a higher salary. It also implies a loss of seniority; the seniority that relates to your choice of schedule—we call it control of your working schedule.

Author: Does the term "where" also imply levels of expectation that are placed on you?

Captain: No. Once a captain, expectations do not change.

The captain went on to explain the relationships between experience and control. The airline prepares a working schedule that is based on seniority at any given level of aircraft. A move from a 737 to a 767 aircraft, for example, is based on seniority flying the 737 aircraft. The new salary is higher, but the rank at the 767 is lower. Also, the level of the captain's control of his work schedule is now low. The starting level of control is where the pilot is "on call." Higher levels of control include receiving regular monthly schedules. These levels may allow the pilot to, as he says, "obtain bids" for taking weekends off, as well as choices of destinations and day versus night flying. On a monthly basis the captain enters what is called a bid package into his computer.

Captain: Quite a bit in the package is standardized. It contains one hundred lines of regularly scheduled trips. Another thirty to thirty-five lines are devoted to reserve/on call schedule.

Author: What about the choice of size of planes you fly in general, not specific aircraft?

Captain: Planes vary in their gross weight capabilities, average flight speeds, and passenger capacities. You use a plane in relationship to your needs.

Author: What about within a given set of characteristics?

The captain's response was long. He spoke about marketing. He gave some examples: "It is cold in the northeastern states in the winter. Demand is high for travel to southern states. And so large planes are chosen for the north-south flow during the winter months." The captain also mentioned fuel efficiency as a factor. "In transcontinental flights, fuel is important and decisions will be made on the basis of size and efficiency."

INDUCTION OF NEW TEAM MEMBERS

Author: You have no say as to who your copilot would be on any given flight. Am I correct?

Captain: The copilot assignment system is identical to that of the pilot assignment system. I have flown with some "one-time copilots" as well as with "several-times copilots." I might fly with the same copilot where we fly together on a two-to-three-day rotation. On the next two-to-three-day rotation in that month I might have a different copilot.

Author: How about the flight attendants?

Captain: Their work schedule is altogether different. It is therefore unusual for a cockpit crew to fly with the same flight attendants.

Author: Do you consider the personnel on the aircraft a team?

Captain: Absolutely.

Author: Are there any formal procedures used to get to know each other?

Captain: Yes. The copilot and I meet formally in the flight operations room prior to going to the aircraft. A standard but an unwritten procedure is that the copilot introduces her- or himself to the captain and not the other way around.

Author: What comes next?

Captain: Usually we talk about the copilot's experiences. The captain sets the tone and the atmosphere. You describe how you behave. That means how you would be running the ship. Soon the conversation moves on to a discussion of emergency situations as well as to normal flight operations.

Author: You mentioned the emergency situation first and then the normal operations.

Captain: Normal operations do not vary much from captain to captain. Handling emergency situations might in terms of what captains want in their capacity as aircraft commanders.
  The captain's head flight attendant is known as the "A line." Here, too, you have a prediscussion, even more so than with the copilot. You need to project the image of leadership and exercise it. You also want to avoid confusion in situations when turbulence is experienced or when mechanical problems occur, or delays, or switching planes, or any other emergency.

Author: Are you expected to do that?

Captain: The A line expects this from you. The rest of the flight attendants expect to hear it from the A line. Briefings are very important, not only for those who do not have much experience, but also for everyone else. We are a team in the aircraft.

Author: A team for the flight!

Captain: That's right. You see, we need to go through a process of induction, not to teach what each role on the aircraft is. Professionals know their own roles. You need the induction in order to get to know me and the copilot and the A line.

Author: Captain, the situation in schools is not the same. Most new personnel come at least for the year. How do you feel about induction of personnel in schools?

Captain: Induction is needed at the beginning of the year but also each time that a new member of the team joins the team.

Author: You mean just the captain with the new member, like you do, or say with the copilot and the A line?

Captain: In schools I think that every time a new staff member comes on board, the principal should have this person get to know everyone else and vice versa.

Author: You mean that a meeting has to be called for that?

Captain: Well, yes. It is not like one flight. It is a team for the whole year, like you said.

Author: Just for my education, Captain, when do you see the A line for the second time?

Captain: When we are ready to go—passengers, luggage, and doors, all is done. She comes to see me. The doors have to be closed and armed. That is for assurances. There is a mechanism there where the doors can slide for escaping purposes. When all is done, the A line comes to me and reports that the doors are closed and armed.

Author: This cannot be done by telephone.

Captain: No, because this is a critical item. That has to be done in person.

At that point the thought crossed my mind about possible commitments that teachers might be giving to the principal at the beginning of the school year. What triggered the thought was how much the captain's leadership accountability depends on the A line's leadership accountability with regard to that door.

PERSONAL RESPONSIBILITY FOR PROBLEMS AND FOR COMMUNICATION

Both the captain and the copilot fly the plane. On the ground, the captain handles security issues, mechanical issues, and unusual issues involving passengers. The captain is the one who taxies the plane. The copilot communicates by radio with air traffic control (ground control and tower control). The captain said, "Informally they each try to anticipate each other's needs. Professionally, both of us are very highly motivated."

The captain sits on the side where the ground steering controls are. Once he is notified by the A line that the doors are closed and armed, the captain taxies under the guidance of the ground control while also listening to the tower. The captain emphasized that he needs to accurately follow both sets of instructions.

Captain: The tower may stop captains, divert them, or let them taxi. The tower gives the release to take off. It is the copilot who continues to talk (a) to the tower by radio, finding out the weather at the destination and (b) to the passengers on the public announcement (PA) system. The tower at the final destination also gives permission to land.

Author: What about communicating with the passengers?

Captain: I might say, "Ladies and gentlemen, the agent has closed the door of the aircraft but there are some last-minute bags. We will be pushing back in four or five minutes."

This reminded me of a year's opening school assembly.

From the gate and up until at least ten thousand feet in the air and down to the arrival gate, below ten thousand feet, the captain flies the plane and the copilot communicates with the tower. The radio is quite busy under ten thousand feet because that is where the majority of all aircraft fly. During a multiday trip the captain may alternate the legs that he and his copilot fly only while the plane is above ten thousand feet. When this happens, the copilot takes all the flight control inputs and makes decisions as to maneuvering the aircraft. But the captain remains the absolute authority at all times, even when the copilot flies the plane and the captain handles radio traffic and other normal copilot duties.

The external guidance of the plane while above ten thousand feet is as follows: Within a five-mile radius of the departing airport, the control tower is "in control." Within a twenty-five-mile radius, another agency ("approach control") issues the instructions. Beyond a twenty-five-mile radius, the Air Route Traffic Control Center takes over. Once the plane reaches the twenty-five-mile radius of the landing airport, the situation is reversed.

Author: When and how do you communicate to the passengers above ten thousand feet?

Captain: Information about the weather and arrival time is very important to our passengers. Also when we reach a point of interest I might say, "Ladies and gentlemen, on the right side of the aircraft we can see the Grand Canyon." On intercontinental flights I may talk about points of interest after having checked with the A line that the movie is over. I do not want to interfere with entertainment. We also provide an aircraft moving-map display to the people in the cabin.

Author: I am interested in your responsibility while your copilot is in control of the aircraft. How do you work together?

Captain: As I said, we alternate above ten thousand feet when there is too much flying on any given day. But the responsibility is mine at any given time. I also must speak from authority.

Author: You mean if a problem occurs and the copilot is in control?

Captain: Yes.

Author: What happens when a problem occurs?

Captain: It depends what kind of problem, of course.

Author: If the copilot is in control do you still consider it your problem?

Captain: Of course. The problems are my responsibility.

The personal responsibility that the captain assumes at all times intrigued me, so I asked, "When a problem occurs and you must communicate its existence to the passengers, how can you say to them that you have already assumed responsibility for the problem even before you are certain about the solution?" The captain did not hesitate at all in answering this question. He began by insisting that he must and always does immediately assume personal responsibility for a problem, the solutions, and the passengers. He does not communicate every problem about which he has taken responsibility to others.

Captain: I am the commander of the aircraft, and everything in it while we travel is my ultimate responsibility. Passengers feel better when they know that I have taken responsibility for a problem that they have become aware of.

Author: Is this a company policy or a philosophy that you have about problems and responsibilities?

Captain: It is so everywhere.

Author: Let me understand. You assume the responsibility for the problem, the solutions, and the passengers. Is that why you feel that you must share information about some problems with the passengers?

Captain: Yes. Sharing information is also part of what I expect myself to do.

Author: Even before the problem has been solved?

Captain: Absolutely, if it has something to do with them. Comfort! Time of arrival! Potential danger! That is the commander's responsibility. I am responsible for explaining what the problem is and informing what is going to be done about it. These two obligations cannot be undertaken without having assumed personal responsibility for the problem. And I must assume this responsibility.

Author: Captain, may I ask you about schools in this regard? Do you think that it should be the same in schools? I mean particularly in relation to problems that occur during the process of achieving goals for the yearlike flights to certain destinations?

Captain: I do not understand why it has to be different than the one in the air. In fact, I assume it is the same.

Author: What if the problem is complex, and it is difficult to come up with a good and possible solution?

Captain: So much more so!

Author: What if you have no control over whatever procedure is employed at the time, like when your copilot is in control or if you have no control, period?

Captain: So much more so! I am the commander of the aircraft. I exercise the control I have, perhaps to the limit. It is my responsibility.

PRIORITIZATION IN TIMES OF SIGNIFICANT PROBLEMS

Author: Can you please identify for me the kinds of problems you encounter and the ways these problems are handled while in the air?

Captain: You are at thirty-five thousand feet going to Atlanta, Georgia, and the weather there is so bad that it seems you have to be diverted to, say, Charleston, South Carolina. I might be able to hold over Atlanta for a while prior to being diverted. How long can I hold? It depends on how much fuel I have and on the passengers' connection times.

Author: [*This sounded familiar to me from schools: mid–school year, learning problems, losing learning time, problems with promotion to the next grade, and what data I need.*] Captain, what kinds of data do you need in such situations, and how do you get the data?

Captain: I coordinate that with the data link to the company operations. The decision is jointly made. We try to balance two, what you may call, negatives— customer inconvenience and fuel cost to the company—without sacrificing safety.

Author: Discomfort in missing flights or just physical discomfort in the plane?

Captain: Both.

Author: How do you measure passengers' inconvenience?

Captain: You make your best estimates.

Author: [*I wondered what competencies school leaders need in order to operate on the basis of such principles.*]

Captain: A rejected takeoff is another sort of a possible problem. When an emergency occurs while the aircraft is already moving, the issue is this: should or could the aircraft be stopped, or should it be allowed to take off to avoid going off the end of the runway and the emergency then be handled after being airborne? The crew is briefed ahead of time about various options and related actions. When something in fact occurs during this phase, decisions are made in a timely manner so as to prevent a greater emergency from occurring.

Author: [*I mused: Stopping the aircraft = not backing off from handling student discipline. Going off the end of the runway = dropping out of school!*] How do you handle other problems?

Captain: All of the other possible problems that might occur in relationship to the operating conditions of the aircraft are handled in accordance with known and practiced procedures, and also there is always prebriefing with the crew. As to turbulence while in the air, it is a normal occurrence. I always prebrief the A line before we fly about expected turbulence based on the weather forecast for our route of the flight.

Author: What about the unexpected turbulence?

Captain: I would make an announcement over the PA system to the passengers. I would also ask the flight attendants to discontinue their meal service and stow away their meal carts and be seated with their seatbelts on. "Safety is paramount," I tell the A line before each flight.

Author: When turbulence starts, what is the role of the A line?

Captain: Turbulence may be perceived differently throughout the cabin. Normally, the very end of the plane receives a more exaggerated effect. This is due to a combination of factors such as wing sweep and relative distance from the wing. I tell her to let me know. If she feels like the turbulence warrants the seatbelt light to be turned on, I am always happy to comply.

When turbulence occurs you worry about safety first. You explain what it is and what to do. When a mechanical problem occurs you need to consider safety first, as well. First, I examine what I can do to correct the problem. Time is of the essence. You need to bring the plane into operating condition as soon as possible and go in the right direction to your destination. In the air force they taught us aviate, navigate, and communicate, in that order.

Author: What exactly is aviating?

Captain: Aviation is manipulating the aircraft flight controls/systems. It is the act of flying the airplane. You must assume responsibility for that above all else.

Author: What is navigating?

Captain: Navigation is the act of maintaining the intended direction, speed, and altitude of the aircraft.

Author: What do you communicate once the solution to the mechanical problem has been found and executed?

Captain: I communicate in brief what was done about it.

Author: How?

Captain: As clearly and as calmly as I can with much assurance either that everything is fine or that we will need to do some more on the ground to correct it but that we are okay until then.

Author: As to passengers, when serious problems occur, what's on your mind, and what do you communicate about besides safety and, as you also said, comfort?

Captain: We always care for the passengers' physical and emotional comfort.

Author: What after that?

Captain: Scheduling and efficiency are important for both the passengers and the company.

Author: Captain, please assume that a major problem is occurring in school. Say, bullying or even armed violence. It is continuing. Everything that needs to be communicated is about to be communicated.

Captain: Thinking and doing whatever can be done about safety. This should be first. Right?

Author: Absolutely, and then what, Captain—comfort, learning schedules, and efficiency, in that order?

Captain: I always think of comfort right after safety. I would want to see it the same way in schools. People need to be provided with physical and emotional support. I am not sure that kids can learn well without it, but I am not an expert on that.

Author: What about trying your best to minimize interferences with the school schedule and not waste learning time?

Captain: I see these both as very important.

Author: Schedules should be ahead of efficiency or the other way around?

Captain: Both are very important.

BEING SCREENED FOR AUTONOMY

To my surprise the captain discontinued his role as a respondent. He started asking me questions! I certainly welcomed that. He asked me what I thought captains have in common with school principals. I suggested that in my opinion both are on a journey, day in and day out. Their career patterns follow the same principles. The division of labor between a captain and copilot basically resembles that which exists between a principal and the assistant principal. I also said that both the captain and the principal are guided by policies.

The captain shared that he has two children attending a semiautonomous charter school.

Captain: In comparison to myself as an aircraft captain, my children's principal assumes too little personal responsibility, particularly in relation to working on preventing problems before they occur.

Author: What do you mean by responsibility in this case, sir?

Captain: In order to be able to take responsibility you have to feel that you are autonomous to do so. School principals should have more autonomy than they do, feel that they have more, and exercise more than they do now.

Author: From what you know, they are not sufficiently autonomous?

Captain: Yes.

Author: Should they be?

Captain: Yes. In fact, they should be screened for autonomy. We are. We are screened very, very carefully over and above the basic knowledge and skills that we are supposed to have. We are screened for being able to meet our job of moving passengers safely to where they wish to go. We need to show that we have autonomy and know how to exercise it, using our power to act whenever it is needed. Why are principals not screened for autonomy? They should be. How else would they risk assuming responsibility for handling problems that occur in the school? Are they the school leaders or not?

I suggested to the captain that I thought autonomy might be dependent, at least in part, on what the school leader is empowered to do, even in a charter school. "I do not mean to defend what exists in schools," I said, "I am just saying what I speculate." The captain responded, "My company does not give me autonomy. My company does not want me to relinquish all of the autonomy I need to make the decisions I have to make. The airline wants me to act autonomously. And they screen me for my ability to act in that way. School leaders should be screened for personal autonomy as well."

Am I detecting arguments based on personal vested interests (his children)? I asked myself. Not knowing for sure, I decided not to continue probing this issue despite my interest in his recommendation. This issue might be at the heart of several other pivotal issues that are involved in the challenge of achieving predetermined school goals. It seems to be extremely important to this aircraft captain, an out-of-the-box perceiver of school leadership, who is task oriented and a rational and clear thinker.

5

Traffic Police Officer Maintains Safety and Enforces the Law

Second on my list of interviewees was a traffic police officer. Of interest to me were the competencies that he possesses and uses in executing his job. I wanted to learn about implications that I might derive for school leaders in the second major challenge: patrolling the school grounds for safety and rule enforcement. I was hoping for recommendations that he might give to help maximize the effectiveness of meeting this challenge in schools.

The interviewee was a twenty-six-year veteran of the police force. He was fifty-six years old and a professionally trained officer who graduated from the California Highway Patrol Academy in Sacramento. He liked what he was doing, he told me, even though he had originally intended to teach school and had earned a lifetime teaching credential for California. At the outset of the interview he emphasized that he did not speak for his department, "Just facts as I know them and just opinions that I personally have."

The officer began by explaining to me that in California all police officers are certified through the Department of Justice. His own experience has been to enforce the law on the roads and to keep them safe. His assignments are primarily on freeways and in unincorporated roads (not city streets). He travels by car (his colleagues in congested, urban areas travel by motorcycle). He receives his assignments based on his choice of being on a regular beat (every day) or on relief (serving when regulars are on their days off). "I like to be on relief. Every day is a new day for me. I like change, but of course, not everyone in the department likes change," he said.

MAXIMUM VISIBILITY IN PROBLEMATIC AREAS

According to this veteran officer, being physically visible on the road is central to law enforcement. "That, in turn, contributes to safety. I warn motorists about a driving hazard, a blind curve, a closed lane, or something else to be aware of, something unusual to expect on the road. Typically, in such situations I may sit in my parked car with my blinking lights on. At other times I stand outside of the car directing traffic. Drivers slow down, and this contributes to safety." Those who drive fast and see him traveling on the road slow down, too. Cars just tend to slow down when he is around.

Officer: While I am traveling on the road I am sometimes able to cover more than one incidence at a time, like where the law is violated or where accidents happen as soon as they have occurred.

Author: You are doing all of this on a full-time basis. As you know, school leaders cannot afford that kind of a time commitment. What would you recommend to school principals insofar as time spent being visible on campus?

Officer: If you are talking about problematic areas, then as much time as possible. This is a top priority. But not all areas are problematic areas.

Author: Officer, in what other activities do you engage?

Officer: I write speeding tickets, other tickets, and reports. I spend time in the car listening with the maximum concentration possible regarding calls for help. At times, pedestrians will stop me when I am parked or stop me when I travel. Some people will ask me for directions or for other kinds of assistance. Other times, I may see pedestrians who seem to have lost their way or others who appear to be in a physical state of needing assistance. In such cases I stop on my own initiative and ask how I can be of help.

Author: You engage in several different activities, sir. When I think of you observing and stopping drivers on the road I also think of principals observing and "stopping" students in school. Please help me see what you look for when you observe?

Officer: Out-of-the-ordinary driving! There are norms of driving vehicles on the road that every driver should abide by. These norms may change, depending on driving conditions and traffic conditions.

Author: What about the clarity of the rules that pertain to more difficult driving conditions?

Officer: They are not as clear as those that pertain to normal driving conditions.

Author: So what do you actually look for?

Officer: I look for situations where there is driving out of the norm. This could easily be characterized as unsafe or suspicious. Weaving around may be one example.

Author: [My imagination focused on what "out of the norm or suspicious" behavior might be in school.] As you are patrolling the road, what is your bottom line regarding the purpose of being visible and knowing how to be visible effectively?

Officer: [without hesitation] You learn to do it all. You should know where you have to be. That is part of your job. You know why you have to be where you have to be. That is also part of your job. You have to know what to look for. You have to be patient. You have to be able to make decisions quickly, to drive cautiously while chasing someone, to concentrate continuously, and to know the law. You are authorized to do all of it, and you are responsible for all of it. You need to act from a position of authority in order to fulfill your responsibility.

Author: Officer, what was that last one?

Officer: Act from a position of authority. You have authority and you have to use it.

COMFORT IN ACTING FROM A POSITION OF AUTHORITY

From that point on in the interview, a great deal of time was spent on the notion of acting from a position of authority. I thought that the best way to learn what the officer was referring to was to ask him to give me some actual examples. I was expecting to first hear about stopping motorists for driving violations and acting as a formal cop. But not so! The officer first brought up examples where he is responding to complaints about illegal parking and requests for help in accident situations.

In the first case, he drives to the appropriate place without turning on his red lights and his siren. Once he verifies the complaint, he orders the driver to move, or in the absence of a driver, he issues a ticket and at times calls for a tow truck to remove the vehicle. "I act with the backing of the law. This is my position of authority," he said. The officer is also called to assist disabled motorists. In accidents where there are injuries or in fatal accidents his authority extends even further. If the accident involves more than one vehicle and he (the officer) is the first to arrive to the scene of the accident, then he would typically call for help.

In the second case, someone else arrives first and calls for help. The officer responds to the call. In case of known injuries, he would speed with his red lights blinking and his siren on. He explained, "What I and other officers do on the scene of the accident itself follows rules, regulations, departmental policies, common sense, and intuition."

At this point in the interview I asked the traffic officer the following questions, hoping to learn more about his responsibility and authority:

- What do you do when you stop a motorist?
- How do you interact with this motorist?

- How do you interact with other individuals in the vehicle if there are any?
- When you feel that you need help, what do you actually do?
- What do you do when you get the help?
- And what do you do if you do not get help?

Officer: Overall, I can say that I am cautious, polite, and I use common sense.

Author: Where is the authority?

Officer: I ordered the motorist to stop, didn't I? And the motorist stopped. He stopped because he knows that I have the authority to stop him.

Author: What do you typically say to drivers that you stop?

Officer: I explain the reason for stopping them. The situation is typically tight. There is sensitivity there. Hearing the reason for being stopped helps to diffuse the situation. This is not exactly acting from a position of authority. It is sensitivity, striving for calmness. It shows that I am comfortable myself acting from authority and being sensitive at the same time.

Author: What happens if there are additional people in the car?

Officer: If the car is full of young men and the stop is for a possible drug or alcohol violation or there is a threatening individual, road rage, or weapon brandishing, then I obviously act quite cautiously. I would typically ask the driver to come out of the vehicle. Once the driver is out of the car, I talk to her or him. The worst situation is when I am confronting weapons.

Author: What about help?

Officer: If I feel that I need help and I can get it quickly, then I pursue it and I do with the driver what I can do. When the help arrives, I brief the officer, we quickly decide on a course of action, and we pursue it.

To act from authority is not being a dictator or being arrogant. It is doing what you think is needed at the moment and that which you have the formal authority to do.

Author: What about a situation where help does not arrive?

The officer provided an example. Once he suspected a contraband situation. Illegal goods were probably being transported, he thought. He followed the vehicle in order to stop it. He then became worried about his own safety. He called for help, and for whatever reason help did not arrive. He then came to a decision "not to carry out the task to completion."

Author: So here you did not even stop the vehicle.

Officer: No, I did not.

Author: You had authority to do this, to not stop it. Right?

Officer: Yes.

Author: Any other examples where you did not stop a vehicle?

Officer: At times it is a small infraction, namely, speeding a bit over the limit. Another case is where the driver exits the freeway into a dense and dangerous urban area. I chase the driver, and I ask for help. Help does not arrive. If I become worried about my own safety, I do not continue to chase the driver.

Author: I do not mean to be disrespectful, but again, deciding not to continue to chase someone is acting from a position of authority?

Officer: Yes, I have the authority to do so, you might say. My own safety is in my hands.

Author: As you speak, my thoughts are also on the school leader. It certainly could happen that a principal might worry about his or her personal safety.

Officer: Well, yes, principals and for that matter everyone else in the school have to be cautious when violence and, especially, armed violence occurs.

Author: Being cautious, then, is also acting from authority?

Officer: Yes. I implied it. It happens even when I am with other law-enforcement officers. We all act with caution from a position of authority.

Author: What about being soft at times? Might that be acting with too little authority?

Officer: I do not think in terms of too little or too much authority.

Author: [*The point, I thought, is to be comfortable with the authority he has and how he uses it.*] In your opinion, when it comes to maintaining safety and enforcing the laws and the rules, should school principals think and act the same as you think and act?

Officer: Yes. Principals, even teachers, anybody, should be comfortable acting from authority if they are charged with rule enforcement. These two things are connected.

Author: You said teachers, too?

Officer: It does not make any difference. The teacher has authority, too. The principal should help the teacher to become comfortable acting from authority if the teacher needs this kind of help.

MAXIMUM COLLABORATION AND MINIMUM CONFUSION IN TIMES OF TROUBLE

Author: Officer, earlier you talked about collaboration. Could you please elaborate? What happens when others are involved in a situation in addition to you?

Officer: Confusion in times of trouble is what you want to minimize and, if possible, eliminate altogether.

Author: What is collaboration?

Officer: Working together. [*He gave an example: He is the first to arrive on the scene. He calls for help on the radio and explains why he needs it. Whoever comes to help learns immediately what the case is.*] Officers feel free to call on any law-enforcement personnel closest to the scene. In a rural area I would call one or more deputy sheriff officers and/or one or more forest rangers. While waiting for help to come I would also act to assure protection. In a riot situation or when a fire erupts, all agencies work together. In an accident on a road in a national forest (a federal jurisdiction), a highway patrolman may come and you could say to him "take it." There could be a range of what we call concurrent relationships.

Author: Where does confusion come in here?

Officer: The key goal is first to reduce confusion of who does what and, if possible, to eliminate confusion altogether.

Author: You said that before. How do you do it?

Officer: By collaborating.

Author: How do you collaborate yet minimize confusion, in accidents, for example?

Officer: First, you assure that nothing worse happens. That is the first responsibility. The second goal is to secure the scene, stabilizing things. You work toward assuring that additional problems do not occur. This is a large part of reducing confusion.

Author: Are you the leader in such a case?

Officer: The fire department and/or an ambulance may arrive before me. If not, then I call them for help when I notice a need for their services. I direct them, and they begin to provide the help needed. It's that logical. Take the case of a rollover. A gasoline tanker overturns, pouring gasoline all over the road. And there is also an injury. You always have to think in terms of priorities.

Author: Like what?

Officer: Hemorrhaging, bleeding, car sideways, blocking freeway, rendering aid—they may all occur or only some of them happen. These are the kinds of things you think about and act on in case of injuries. Several things happen at the same time. A range of things needs to be taken care of. And you always think of who else can help. That's when collaboration comes in.

Author: And what about your own leadership role, especially in relationship to others, not just individuals but agencies as well?

Officer: In an accident situation, again, if I call for help and it comes soon then I call the shots. I am what we call the "scene manager." Federal and state regulations specify that the scene manager is, by definition, the one who has responded first. This manager possesses the authority to tell others what to do. I assume control of things. I may decide, for example, to close lanes for the safety of the firemen and the ambulances.

Author: Are you always the one who "calls the shots" and on all issues in such cases?

Officer: No. In complex situations, somebody else calls the shots. A person arrives on the scene and serves as the incidence response supervisor.

Author: Would that be like, in our case, a law-enforcement individual arriving at the school or possibly a superintendent speaking with a school principal on the phone?

Officer: You might say so. Whoever it is, this person establishes a central command. She or he may come from the ranks of the highway patrol (state) or the city police. The supervisor takes charge of everything, including such things as calling for health inspectors in the face of hazardous material, for example.

Author: Help me out please. What would you say about who is in charge, about collaboration, and about confusion if law-enforcement personnel are already on the school campus?

Officer: You will have to be more specific.

Author: Sure, as soon as I become an expert myself on maintaining safety and enforcing the law.

We laughed a bit and spent some time chatting informally about a variety of things unrelated to the purposes of the interview.

HELP OTHERS TO ACT FROM A POSITION OF AUTHORITY

Author: Given the need to pursue the challenges you face in collaboration with others, allow me to come back to the notion of acting from authority.

Officer: Fine. It is important, very important.

Author: We talked before about confusion and collaboration in times of trouble. And before that you had suggested that a principal might be able to help teachers to be comfortable acting from a position of authority. Have you ever helped somebody under you to become comfortable acting from authority?

Officer: Absolutely, and others have helped me years back. But I am not sure that this has anything to do with people under you or people above you. It has to do with people who are comfortable acting from a position of authority helping those who lack but need that comfort.

AWARENESS OF ALL THAT IS OCCURRING WHEN LAW-ENFORCEMENT PERSONNEL ARE ON THE SCENE

I returned to the topic of law-enforcement personnel being on campus.

Author: In such a case, officer, can we at least talk about possible issues?

Officer: Everyone involved has to know the law.

Author: In your opinion, what kind of law and how much of the law should a school principal know?

Officer: As much as possible: what, why, and possible results. All the ones that are involved need to be on the same wavelength when police come to schools. Look, if we in law enforcement do not collaborate with other personnel when the situation calls for it, we get a ticket, a reprimand, from our own commanders. I do not know about principals. You cannot use the excuse of not knowing the law for not collaborating with the police. In my opinion, the principal should know what is happening, the causes and the consequences.

Author: Can you please give me an example or two again?

Officer: Think of a belligerent person and think of experiencing difficulties and calling for help as a result. The agency that is called must come to help. Think of a gas main pipe that ruptures in a construction site due to high pressure, and there are difficulties handling it. The agency that is called for help must respond. Or, think about a situation when a fire-department commander calls for help to close a road, then I must respond. But whoever is there has to know the law as it pertains to what I may or may not do, what they may do or may not do.

Author: If law-enforcement personnel do not come to school, do they get a ticket too?

Officer: Yes. This is considered not helping, lack of collaboration, not doing what you are supposed to do.

Author: How would you feel if you came to a school to help? Would you see yourself as the "site supervisor"?

Officer: When I interact with a motorist, I am the boss. Even when I patrol for safety, I am a boss. When I am first to arrive on the scene of an accident, I engage in leadership. In school, to a certain extent, I also am a leader, but the principal is the overall leader.

EASE OF INTERPRETING AND APPLYING DISTRICT AND SCHOOL RULES

This interview was not going in a very orderly manner. Some topics were cut short and reappeared later on. Others were discussed in great length, perhaps too long. But since maintaining safety and enforcing rules are so important in schools, I persevered. Over three hours passed; I was exhausted. He was not. I did not feel quite satisfied. I did not feel that I could easily summarize the knowledge, skills, and aptitude that I had heard him say he was using in pursuing his challenge. Continuously, of course, I had in mind the principal patrolling the school grounds. I was looking for the specialized competencies involved.

Author: With your permission, officer, may I reiterate what I heard you suggest directly and indirectly to school principals as they patrol the school grounds for safety and rule enforcement?

Officer: Sure.

Author:

- Spend as much time as possible engaging in patrolling.
- Look for out-of-the ordinary situations.
- Respond when asked for help.
- Provide help when observing a need for it.
- Act comfortably from a position of authority.
- Help others become comfortable acting from authority.
- Be cautious.
- Be polite.
- Collaborate with other people and agencies when needed.
- Minimize confusion.
- Work with supervisors.
- Be aware of what is going on when law-enforcement personnel are on the scene.
- And know the law.

Officer: Sounds fine, but did I say all that? I would add intuition. Using intuition is very important when safety is in jeopardy or when a problem erupts or when a law is violated.

Author: Could you please share with me under what conditions in your work does intuition play an important role?

Officer: This would apply when there are uncertainties in the rules. Interpreting would be difficult. But it is a must. Principals have to know and understand the rules that they have to work with. Your intuitive actions have to be based on this knowledge. Then you need to be able to properly inform and often interpret the rules to others.

Author: Could you elaborate on that?

Officer: When the fire department, an ambulance, a Cal Trans worker, and I are responding to an accident, each one of us knows the policies and rules we personally work with. We also know our roles and what is expected of each one of us in a given case. If I need anything specific from any one of them, they know exactly what I mean, and they comply immediately. Everybody's intuition seems to match each other's. Everyone agrees to compromises about interpreting some rules.

The police officer went on to explain how in each case the leader uses intuition to help achieve those compromises.

Officer: This is Esprit de Corps.

Author: From what you personally know about school principals, do you think that they have the ability to succeed in times of trouble in interpreting and implementing rules?

Officer: Truthfully, I am not sure. I know principals work very hard, and I feel sorry for them. Part of their and our problem is how to minimize and eliminate confusion when you have to do what you have to do. This has to be learned and practiced. I would like to see it in schools. A lot of it has to do with starting with rules that are known and using them to go further.

Author: Can you think of a relevant hypothetical case where this would apply in a school?

Officer: Oh, think of a case when an officer comes in. City officers would know more than I do about it. We already talked about it. But, say, there is "carrying of a weapon." It could be a knife. There is also "under the influence." There is "assault." A simple one-punch assault with a serious injury may happen, resulting in a broken bone. This is a "felony." The law says that the kid has to be taken away, even though the school authorities may not like it. Also, the parents have to be notified because we are talking about juveniles. And of course you think of the injured and others, not just about fear but shock and more. Then there are also parents of other kids.

Author: Where in your opinion should the school district come in here?

Officer: The district should set the rules with regard to as many possible incidences that it can think of (if it has not done that yet). The policies should be easy for the principal to understand and interpret to others. This should be done not just for procedures related to suspensions but also for procedures that are relevant to every conceivable situation. It would be nice to see the district, the schools, and law-enforcement personnel on the same wavelength. Responding to student misbehavior must never be left to uncertainty.

Author: Have you other thoughts?

Officer: We got lost in details. Let's not forget that patrolling for safety is proactive. It detects problems early. As much time as possible should be devoted to it.

Author: Do you have any other ideas for school principals in particular?

Officer: This is corny but true: they should be the cheerleaders of their schools.

6

Crop Grower Maximizes Yield per Unit of Cost

This chapter features a summary of an interview with the third professional, a crop grower. The relevance of his competencies to school leaders
pursuing the third challenge, I thought, would be high. Principals need to
enhance the benefits their students accrue in school. The crop grower does
the same with plants. The two professions produce graduates and har-
vested crops. Both make decisions associated with the processes that lead
to these products.

My interview was with a production manager in a large plant-growing
company. This man had served previously as a pesticide control officer in
another company. He was forty-six years of age at the time and possessed a
BA degree in agronomy. He said to me that he loved his work, loved the
"challenges that come with the job." At the beginning of the interview, I
asked him what were his overall responsibilities in the company.

Grower: I do two things. One is participating with other department heads in
the annual decision making about what to grow. The other, a major one, is
[*that*] with the help of my staff I am involved in the actual growing of the crop
and particularly in problems that interfere with the growth of our plants. I do
this all year long.

Author: Could we first talk about interferences?

Grower: Certainly. This is my department's major duty.

MAXIMIZING GROWTH BY
MINIMIZING INTERFERENCE WITH IT

Growing plants and minimizing interferences with their growth require, according to this department manager, "simply knowledge and skills in the science and management of growing plants. The company's overall priorities, including its resources and efficiency considerations, are quite significant as well."

Within the context of the challenge school leaders face of enhancing student benefits per given unit of cost, that statement's analogies would be curriculum and pedagogy, administration, and considerations of resources and their use.

In planning for planting and in the preparation of the soil, choices of schedules are a key factor. The actual schedules in this company are prepared by one of the owners and given to the planting department and the ranch managers to implement. The production department does the actual cultivation of the plants. Fundamental choices associated with cultivation are the same for all crops. The choices include

- planting the seeds;
- fertilizing and watering the seeds;
- germinating (observing the seeds "coming alive," emerging from the ground);
- watching growth;
- analyzing soil samples from around the plant's roots in the laboratory to determine the level of nutrients;
- making decisions about whether or not to add nutrients and, if so, how much (different plants require different fertilizers, and there is a need to take into account the requirement to keep ground water clean);
- fertilizing again, if needed, within twenty to thirty days (cannot wait any longer than that); and
- watering while taking into account the need to avoid flooding and soil erosion.

I asked about his needed competencies.

Grower: Those skills are acquired with experience in observing the whole process as well as in individual cases. In this way you minimize mistakes. To be aware of mistakes you have to be able to apply fundamental knowledge of biology, mathematics, basic computer literacy, and the ability to converse with others.

Author: Why converse with others?

Grower: Because people see things from different vantage points, and ultimately you have to make the best choices.

Author: Are the mistakes the only problems?

Grower: We do not always know for sure.

He mentioned problems associated with plant growing or what he referred to as interferences with growth. Regarding what I thought are considerations that might be of interest to school leaders, I asked him about issues he encounters in the following general areas:

- harvesting the maximum possible yield per acre (maximizing learning benefits per cost);
- minimizing interferences at the different stages of growth (minimizing learning problems);
- determining readiness for harvest (assessing potential for promotions and graduation); and
- preparing the field for the next round of cultivation (working on curriculum).

The grower considered harvesting as the overall production of outcome. He began with the topic of interferences, insects, and diseases. I was thinking of children's broken homes, students' learning disabilities, and discipline issues. I immediately (too soon) thought of solutions to problems, such as diagnosing correctly, remedial work, mentoring, special services, extra personnel, and the funding of such activities.

Grower: Insects and diseases damage the crop. We have five licensed pest-control people who patrol the field. They look for interferences with growth and make recommendations about how to handle the problems. I make the final decisions.

Author: Could you please elaborate?

Grower: The key goals are to preserve the crop and to calculate the estimated yield loss (forgone benefits) that is sufficient to offset the cost of the corrections.

Author: How do you achieve these goals?

Grower: The major criterion for determining the yield of the crop, or what we call the last vestige, is the relationship between supply and demand. The return per unit is very much related to whether the ground is owned, bought, or rented. The idea is always to increase the yield at a given cost. But in urban areas the costs associated with the ground itself play more of a role than they do in rural areas.

I thought of building new schools because of growing enrollment and, conversely, closing schools because of shrinking enrollment, decreasing state general aid because of shrinking average daily attendance, large transportation costs per student in rural areas, and other issues.

Author: How about an example?

Grower: There are about fifty types of lettuce heads. We test what looks better, what holds up to disease better, what yields better. We try two thirty-seven-inch-wide beds, one next to the other instead of each one separately. If we get 33 percent more yield, then we are doing fine. We economize. We place plants closer to each other but not too close so that air can flow freely. We irrigate right. We dry. We cultivate before we water again. We leave room for plants to breath, as I said. We kill weeds.

Author: [*Sounds somewhat like class size, individual differences, zero-tolerance policies, and so forth, I thought. But they still control what to grow. We do not.*] Now please tell me a bit about the readiness for the harvesting and harvesting itself.

Grower: A separate department does that.

Author: No help or guidance from your department?

Grower: Well, they can estimate time needed to harvest the broccoli, for example. Estimated time is known from history. Mother nature plays a role too, however. That is why they have to walk the broccoli fields, observe, and estimate. They have to do it more than once. We get involved when pesticides are needed. Harvesting can take place no earlier than two weeks after that.

Author: And what about getting ready for the next round? Here, it turns out, additional competencies are needed.

Grower: Celery, for example, should not be planted on the same ground more than twice in a row. Another one is about crop rotation. It serves not only as a precaution for the crop but also a must for the soil. You learn on the basis of what you know from previous times and from the ones before it and from the ones before that and so forth. You learn how to maximize the yield without significantly increasing the cost.

Author: Sir, it seems to me that as a production manager you are familiar with so many aspects of the production process and, specifically, with the efforts taken to minimize the various kinds of interferences with production. We might say that schools also produce—educated people, that is, not plants—and that principals are production managers, maybe leaders in the production process. There are many learning problems in schools.

Given your specialty and experience, what would you recommend first and foremost to school leaders to do?

Grower: In my company I am accountable for the overall production process. They should be so, too. On a more detailed level, they need to see learning problems as interference with growth. By their nature, such problems threaten the learning outputs. You do not want to have less. You want more learning, better learning, and greater success in and out of school. They should be familiar with and involved in providing remedies to learning problems and minimizing these problems decisively, authoritatively, and efficiently.

MARKETING PRODUCTS

"Salability," the crop grower says, is "the major consideration associated with marketing products." Predictions have to be made about how well the crop can be both marketed and sold. He first outlined issues related to the basic plants. In his company, basic plants include head lettuce, spinach, and asparagus. "What does 'basic' mean?" I asked, and thought about "regular" students.

Grower: It includes what you typically grow. The company's assumption is that if nothing of significance changes in the demand for the crop, we grow it. The company continues to grow the basic, the same plants.

Author: What about how much to grow of the same crop? [*I thought of amount of learning, not of students over which school leaders have no control.*]

Grower: When it comes to choices related to quantity, comparisons are made with the previous two years.

Author: Which data are looked at and why two years?

Grower: Two years are a better predictor than one year. Choices of data include quantities cultivated, income, quantities of unsold crop, and finding out what is needed out there. These are the key considerations. Choices about how much of the basic plants and whether or not to go for other plants for the coming year are based on integrating all of this information together.

My mind focused on grade-level promotions again and also on graduation rates. I thought of dropout rates, the curriculum, achievement test scores, and fast and slow learners. When I came to cost, I asked whether his department has a self-contained budget for what it contributes to the production process.

Grower: We do most of the time.

Author: [*Since most school principals control only a small portion of the school expenditures, I asked him the following:*] Do you see any comparability between your responsibility in the department and the school principal's responsibility?

Grower: Oh boy. You want to get me started? I am having a hard time hiring good people. It is the school's duty, utmost duty, to prepare kids for college and for jobs. I mean the curriculum, the basics, and the specializations. And I mean the tests, the intermediate ones and the ones at the end.

I wanted to cool down the atmosphere so I asked about the company. My interviewee told me that six individuals own the company. This particular company has been a family farm for over seventy years. The owners are very involved in the day-to-day operations. There is a general manager who spends quite a bit of time on safety issues. He meets every Monday with five department heads, including production, planting, harvesting, marketing, and cooling (in storage and transportation vehicles), and four ranch managers. They review matters and make decisions, if needed.

The head of the production department works in close contact with other departments about what to grow, but especially with the marketing department. Often the company will try new products. Examples include different kinds of lettuce or different vegetables or organic types of crop. Some risks are involved in such cases, but there are also major benefits.

For obvious reasons, I imagined school leaders as ranch managers, and teachers as ranchers. I was interested in learning more about the specific roles and about the authority relationships that the production manager has with them. I assumed that market conditions dictated these relationships.

Grower: Ranch managers treat the ranches as if they owned them. They are the real growers. They put in a seventy-hour workweek.

Author: Are the relations within your department formal ones?

Grower: Yes, but quite socializing as well. There is lots of informality. There are feelings of a family. I think it is due to the fact that the owners are open.

Author: Is there anyone among those involved in the production processes who talks about the products, marketing them and making profits for the company?

Grower: Oh, yes! The ranch owners do.

Author: [*At that point, I decided to come back with caution to the topic of the responsibility of school principals regarding marketing products of schools.*] Do you think that it is good that ranch managers talk to workers about products and marketing?

Grower: Yes.

Author: But what if there are problems with the products?

Grower: Still, that is important.

Author: What about inability to improve something or even mistakes?

Grower: No finger pointing whatsoever. Everyone believes that you need to fix a little problem before it becomes bigger. My department and I are always aware of it, and the ranch managers are quite cooperative. We end up fixing problems together.

Author: Is every single problem fixable?

Grower: Well, one way or another!

Author: Do you think that every learning problem in school is fixable so that the product would be suitable for marketing?

Grower: Well, it is up to the teachers and the principals.

Author: Can they fix it all?

Grower: They can improve the students' readiness. Look! Our ranch managers manage the ranches, and I manage the production in all of the ranches. It is the duty of all of us to minimize interference with plant growth for marketing purposes. The owners hire us and empower us to market the best possible products as long as we understand what the company is all about. Schools should do the same.

Author: Do ranch managers know about harvesting and marketing and making profits?

Grower: As production people, we help in this area.

The thought of a possible comparable role for school district personnel entered my mind. How could the challenge school leaders face about enhancing student benefits with fixed resources be pursued without setting learning standards that relate to what school graduates are able to do? So I asked,

Author: You are not only interacting with ranch managers, but you are also serving as a link between the production people and the marketing people. Am I right?

Grower: Yes. You might view me in that way. It makes sense.

Author: Would you suggest to school leaders to act in such capacities as well?

Grower: I sure wish, but who is the producer in school? Who does the marketing? To be a link you need to have things or people to link with.

Author: What would you suggest?

Grower: I will tell you. Students do not know enough science and mathematics. Some do not know how many feet are in a mile. Many cannot calculate without a calculator. And then you need English. Many students cannot spell without a spell-check. Students need to learn the love of work, too. They need to learn to respect others. They need to learn to be indebted and to have gratitude and to develop a direction in which they want to go. They need the basics.

Author: Yes, many people agree with a lot of what you say.

Grower: I mean academic basics, psychological basics, and social basics. School graduates need not only to get jobs. They also need to learn while on the job, becoming better workers and happier people. Those who run schools should push and push and push to that end, too.

Author: You mean push the students or perhaps also the teachers, the school district, or those who provide jobs, or the college admission officers?

Grower: I do not push plants. All I can do is contribute toward maximizing the quantity and quality of the crop and making profits from selling it by pushing myself. You are responsible for detecting and minimizing interferences with growth here and learning problems in the school. You do not turn your back to them. That's the key. Don't turn your back to problems.

Author: Who is "you" in school?

Grower: The principal.

Author: So growing crops for you is problem solving?

Grower: No. It is maximizing crop yield for marketing and minimizing interferences with its growth. It is also setting it all up for production.

Author: Would you say the same about educating students in schools?

Grower: Yes. Absolutely.

7

Automobile Service Advisor Solves Problems

He starts his weekday at 5:15 A.M. with not a small, not a "grande," but a "venti" cup of coffee. This thirty-two-year-old is not a school leader, but his day is at least as hectic, if not more so, than the day of a principal. That is because his job is, as he says, "to face the challenge of helping people take care of problems that are solvable so life can keep moving along." I interviewed him in great length about this challenge and how it relates to the comparative challenge for the school leader. "Yours is a high-pressure job, is it not?" He answered, "You have to be as efficient as you can and as human as you can at the same time."

I had earlier observed him twice for an hour each time. The pressure is there, no question about it. The pressure originates from the knowledge that there are a lot of problems that have to be solved simultaneously and that despite the fact that he does not control it all, he is the customers' contact for solving these problems.

To him, regardless of the result, every problem to which he attends is a minor one because, as he says, "it is fixable." That is his philosophy. Many problems that come before the school leader are also fixable, but would school leaders call them minor? Surely, not all of those fixable problems could be labeled minor. But it was this philosophy of his that intrigued me (that anything that is fixable is minor). It influenced my choice of questions throughout the interview. I wanted to know what specialized competencies are needed to help solve "minor" problems. I also wanted to know what would be considered major problems.

My interviewee is a service advisor in an automobile dealership. He is a high school graduate. He has been doing this kind of work for nine years, moving a few times, each time to a larger place. His service department includes eighteen technicians. I asked him if he received any training for this work.

Service Advisor: I took a few weekends to sit in executive development workshops. The owner sent me.

Author: Are you content with your work?

Service Advisor: I am happy with my work, but not completely happy, not completely satisfied.

Author: [*I did not ask him why. Next I asked him about his qualifications for his job*].

Service Advisor: Day in and day out work! That is my major qualification. That is also what my work is all about. Day in and day out experience, that is my learning. You accumulate hands-on experiences. Every day is different. You learn as you go along. I got my education gradually. I went from providing services for two or three cars a day to dozens a day. While doing it all I also went from selling a thirty-five-dollar car wax job to selling a fifty-thousand-dollar automobile. My education has depended on the place in which I worked—starting in a car wash and now in a most highly and efficiently organized car dealership. During the years, my bosses have always helped me a lot. Each helped me in different ways.

REFLECTING ON DECISIONS AND ON HOW TO COMMUNICATE THEM

Author: You are the most sought-out advisor in the service department here. Why? How do customers and you get together?

Service Advisor: Who told you that? What do you mean "getting together"?

Author: Let me ask you this: When someone comes to you with a need, do you see a customer there? A client? A car? A problem? Sorry if I am confusing you, but I know that you are not a technician.

Service Advisor: That's okay. It is very simple. I see everything.

Author: But, if you would please, in a couple of words, tell me what do you really see.

Service Advisor: I see friends. All of my customers are my friends.

Author: What?

Service Advisor: Yes. People call me or come in to see me for ongoing service or for taking care of a problem. If they get out of here satisfied, they become my friends.

Author: Are they becoming regular customers, too?

Service Advisor: You bet.

Author: How can they be friends and customers at the same time?

Service Advisor: They can be both if you have taught yourself to make correct technical and financial decisions and arrangements and if you have taught yourself how to communicate everything right.

Author: How do you teach yourself all that?

Service Advisor: You teach yourself how to reflect about what you face and your relationship to what you face.

Author: Wow, that is heavy. What do you mean?

Service Advisor: Every customer has a different problem. Every customer is a different human being. What you want to achieve at the end is to satisfy both. You help solve the problem, and you make the customer happy.

Author: Does that create friendship?

Service Advisor: You bet.

Author: You know that I am here because of my interest in education and, specifically, because the school principal is not doing the teaching, yet people often come to the principal when they have problems. Would you recommend to principals to adopt your philosophy and strategies?

Service Advisor: I know about them! I was in their office a lot when I was a student, but I did not come to them, they called me in.

Author: [*My approach was too hasty, I felt. So I shifted to specifics.*] With what kinds of problems do customers-turned-friends come to you?

Service Advisor: Just a minute. Not everyone becomes a friend, only the satisfied ones. The major types of needs include the following:

- prevention service,
- maintenance service, and
- detection of problems or potential problems.

Author: I suppose the first thing you might do is diagnose the problem.

Service Advisor: Here is when people and problems come together. I diagnose both. I have five kinds of customers. "What kinds of people," you might ask. Right? The first I designate as "number 1." This customer comes for a repair job. The job is done but goes sour. The customer comes back upset. The problem is corrected. The customer, mind you, comes back to us rather than go elsewhere from then on.

Author: Why do you label this customer as number 1?

Service Advisor: To this customer I am committed, and this customer knows that even when I tried to help and it was not sufficient, I would do the best that I can.

Author: Who else?

Service Advisor: Another "number 1" is an employee of the dealership.

Author: Before you go on, does that mean that not everyone is equal?

Service Advisor: We are fair to everyone, but hear me out.

Author: Sorry.

Service Advisor: A "number 2" customer is a regular. He gives an okay to do what we say has to be done. He is appreciative. "Number 3" is the regular customer who comes for warranty purposes only. This is important to the manufacturer—that the service is good. "Number 4" is a fairly regular customer who makes an appointment for anything that she or he needs.

Author: Do you prefer that?

Service Advisor: Well, it depends on several things. How busy we are and so forth. Lots of people just come in, just show up.

Author: Who is your "number 5"?

Service Advisor: Number 5 is an "out-of-towner," a first-timer who comes without an appointment.

Author: So, now, can you please tell me the sum total of combining people and problems?

Service Advisor: The more I learn about the person, the easier it is for me to communicate with this person about any problem that she or he comes with, even if the problems vary greatly (which they do).

Author: So, is that what you meant before? Is it that you spend time thinking what and how to communicate to a customer about a problem? Is it that it depends not only on the problem but also on the person we are talking about?

Service Advisor: Yes.

Author: Please let me know: would you recommend this for school principals?

Service Advisor: What is "this"?

Author: Sorry. I mean the close relationships between the problems, the people, the decisions, and how to communicate the decisions.

Service Advisor: Yes, I would recommend that.

Author: Including the communication about the cost of fixing problems?

Service Advisor: Yes, the cost is part of a car problem and a person problem. That is why it is also a decision problem and a communication problem.

Author: I had assumed that costs of parts and labor are standardized.

Service Advisor: Yes, they are, but I am speaking of the meaning of these costs.

MARKETING SERVICES

Author: Please forgive me, but I have so many more questions to ask you. I would really appreciate learning as much as you can teach me about this whole dynamic, that is, your interactions with other people. The time you spend thinking about how to communicate decisions. For example, what do you do when a regular customer comes in for an ongoing service for the car and you happen to detect a problem with the car? [*I was thinking about a person coming to the principal to arrange or coordinate something and the principal immediately detecting that there is a bigger problem there.*] Do you try to help prevent a problem from happening?

Service Advisor: Now you forgive me, please. You are trying to think of too much at once. You ask questions where the answers depend on specific situations. A priori valid answers I cannot give you. It does not work this way. A lot of it grows with you as you learn more and more from situations: when to call in a technician, for example, or when to ask the customer to stay for a few minutes until the problem becomes clearer.

Author: What helps you to do that?

Service Advisor: No matter what, 90 percent of my job is listening. Almost nothing but my listening takes place at the beginning of an interaction with a customer.

Author: Like saying nothing after "how can I help you"?

Service Advisor: We provide almost any kind of service that exists to almost everyone who comes for service. I help people understand that. I don't only solve problems. I market ourselves all the time.

Author: [*He reoriented me to his scale of the five kinds of customers and their problems*].

Service Advisor: With the number 5 and number 3 customers, I am quick to answer. We diagnose the problem with number 5, and explain it to this out-of-towner. We provide information about a car rental, and we do the service. The number 3 customer comes in to have work done under a warranty. That is all that we do, and that is what we say we can do. We often repeat a couple of times what we do. This is another way we market our services.

Author: What about the other types of customers?

Service Advisor: As I said, with the other customers, we listen to what they tell us. Once you know what's wrong, you want the customer to learn about it, too. When I am done with explaining what we are going to fix, I say, "Can I offer you a ride?" or, "Do you need a car for today?"

Author: Do you cut off the interaction?

Service Advisor: I am done when I feel that I am done, and it is good for the customer to be done. Sure, we are all busy, but talking too long about something [*when*] you know what it is and what will be done to take care of it is not very useful.

Author: Do you ever worry that once a customer hears what the problem is and what the cost will be, she or he will go elsewhere for service?

Service Advisor: This is always a possibility. They may have gone elsewhere first, too, but I can easily tell. It is seldom the cost. Rather, it is not having sufficient confidence that the problem will be taken care of.

Author: Excuse me, but are you doing a sales job on me now?

Service Advisor: Why do I have to do that? You are here already.

Author: [*I was interested in cost and choice of place for service issues.*] Still, is it not true that cost is an issue sometimes and that a customer might go elsewhere after having talked to you?

Service Advisor: Well, that is somewhat complex. Maybe we should move on.

Author: Is it a matter of confidentiality?

Service Advisor: It is a matter that involves options such as doing the minimum or more and how much more—or using one type of part or another, et cetera. Let me ask you this: isn't it true that sometimes people are unhappy with the principal, and they go to the superintendent? To solve what they need may be costly. Sometimes what is important to them is who they hear it from.

Author: [*I became silent.*]

Service Advisor: You need to find out how interested the customer is. Does she or he understand it? But remember, you should not talk too much, cost and other things. You need to give the information but talk as little as possible. If you talk too much, the customer may really get scared. They may possibly go to a supervisor. They could go elsewhere for service. They might even decide not to have the car taken care of, which actually might lead to more serious things, such as unsafe driving and accidents. Talking too much increases options for the customer without the customer understanding the costs. You need to listen, examine, decide, communicate, answer questions, and say, "Have a good day."

Author: What else?

Service Advisor: You should never forget that it is the customer who came in with the problem, not you.

Author: Sure.

Service Advisor: You should not forget that you should gain the customer's trust. The customer should be comfortable shopping in your service department.

Author: What about help for you?

Service Advisor: I do not need much, but at times I do need it. I estimate time, and I estimate cost of parts and labor. There is a flat rate per hour for repair work. We assign a job to a particular technician based on the technician's specialty.

The specialties include

- suspension and brakes,
- transmissions,
- heavy line work (engine),
- drivability,
- electric and air conditioning,
- lube and oil, and
- bumper to bumper.

Service Advisor: The dispatcher who works with me does the assignment of jobs to specific technicians. He also writes the repair orders. The dispatcher is an extremely experienced person. I do not order the parts. The technicians do. This is the way it is here. It is a good system, an efficient system, a friendly system.

Author: About other points with regard to how you help solve problems, I have additional questions if I may.

Service Advisor: Please go ahead.

Author:

- How do you, if at all, monitor the progress of a particular job?
- What are some possible reasons for calling the customer before the job is completed?
- How do you say what you need to say to the customer in such a circumstance?
- Please describe the various interactions you may have with a customer after the job is completed.
- And what about interactions with a customer later on with regard to the original problem, if at all?

Service Advisor: I try to find out at what stage each of my jobs is. I do not intimidate anyone, but I like to be correct in my time estimates. One of the main reasons for calling a customer before a job is completed is that the automobile will be ready later than promised.

Author: What would you typically say then?

Service Advisor: I simply say that an additional unexpected time for the repair is needed.

Author: And then?

Service Advisor: Will it kill you if the car spends the night here?

Author: And then?

Service Advisor: The answer might be "no." Then I offer them a rental car with a large discount, if they wish. If the answer is "yes" and "why," et cetera, then I go into detail explaining what has been done, found, and still needs to be done. These things occur when there are big jobs.

Author: Is it hard to communicate these kinds of things?

Service Advisor: What do you want me to say: "Have mercy on me" or, "This is tough"?

Author: Can you describe your interactions with a customer after a job has been completed?

Service Advisor: I call. I say that the job is done. I see to it that the car is washed if there is a sign to do it (a "hat" placed on the roof). In the end I see to it that the customer is completely satisfied. When your job is to help solve problems, this is what it is all about—customer satisfaction.

DECISION FROM THE HEART

Author: School leaders also learn from experience.

Service Advisor: I am sure they do.

Author: They also might see a problem and a person and they listen.

Service Advisor: I know that some of the problems in schools are assigned to assistant principals or teachers or specialists.

At that point the automobile service advisor and I began a conversation about the similarities between his role and the principal's role and his role in helping to solve problems. He agreed that to help solve problems all day long is tough in both places because of the pressure.

Service Advisor: At times, I ask myself, "How long can I present such a calm demeanor?"

Author: Indeed, how long?

Service Advisor: As long as I myself feel calm.

Author: What are the factors that help you remain calm?

Service Advisor: Personality, you might say.

Author: Is there anything else or anything more specific? I am trying to learn about your specialized competencies so that I can share them with school leaders.

Service Advisor: I am not qualified to suggest anything to school leaders about what they should do. All I can tell you is what skills I think I have.

Author: You mentioned some. Could you give me an overview, please?

Service Advisor:

- Empathy
- Communication skills

- Decision-related skills, how to make them, and how to share them
- Marketing skills

When I went to school, not everyone really listened. Maybe they listened, and I thought that they did not. I don't know. But I will tell you, I have several customers who are what you call "leaders" in schools—principals and assistant principals, I suppose. But they do not have enough sales ability, no sir!

Author: Do you mean salesmanship?

Service Advisor: No. Salesmanship is being there in order to sell and also influence the customer. Sales ability is offering something for sale that really fits the need of a customer.

Author: How do you do that?

Service Advisor: You sell from the heart.

Author: [*I said nothing.*]

Service Advisor: Your school people do not listen or speak enough from the heart—not enough from the heart!

Author: How is "sales ability" related to "from the heart"?

Service Advisor: You make decisions all day. When you make a decision it has to be a decision in which you truly believe. You believe that it is as close as possible to what the customer needs. This kind of a decision comes from the mind all right, but it has to also come from the heart.

Author: Is it an issue of a balance between the mind and the heart?

Service Advisor: You want to hear about automobiles or schools?

Author: Schools.

Service Advisor: When I was younger, I knew only a little bit about the people you call school leaders. The school leaders whom I know now I know quite well. Sure you have to make decisions from your mind and from your heart. You also have to be sure that those that are affected by your decision are convinced in their mind and in their heart that it is the right decision. I know that it is not easy to do it with kids, but you have to work on it. Try working with teachers and parents first when they come to complain.

I had not thought about the mind-heart balance quite in that way before: the problem solver and the one with the problem both have a mind and a heart with regard to the problem and the solution. Each of them plays a "balance game." Perhaps this man talked from his own school experience. Does he see a third balance, I wondered, the balance between the two balances. I wanted to continue, but I could tell that he was ready to close the conversation. I thanked him. Then he said, "It is hard for me to explain. You understand that I cannot share with you specific cases. These are private matters."

But I knew that the pertinence of the ideas this advisor has and the methods he uses to implement them would have to be examined with school leaders themselves. At that point in the interview I was not quite sure what I could or would share about this interview with school leaders.

8

Chief Financial Officer Assumes Fiduciary Responsibility

Fiduciary responsibility is structured differently in different school districts. Accounting for some of the differences are different administrative traditions, different means of financial support, and different authority relationships. School leaders must work in accord with district financial guidelines and together with pertinent personnel at the district office level. And all of this is done within the context of state and federal fiscal laws and mandates.

School leaders have only partial discretionary financial powers. But they are continuously challenged with fiduciary responsibility in their school. School leaders almost always remark that, as leaders of schools in (nonprofit) school districts, their discretionary financial powers are limited. Close examinations reveal variability among leaders and schools with regard to several dimensions of fiduciary responsibility. There are differences in accounting and auditing skills, budgetary knowledge, efficiency-related aptitudes, and reporting-related competencies.

In order to learn about the challenge of assuming at least one kind of fiduciary responsibility, I interviewed a specialist whose whole job is pursuing this role. The interviewee served at the time as the chief financial officer (CFO) in another nonprofit organization, a medical rehabilitation institute. Both the institute and a school are funded by categorical (earmarked) and by noncategorical (general) financial sources.

At the time of the interview, the CFO had had thirteen years of service in nonprofit health service institutions. He was fifty-three years of age, with formal undergraduate and graduate training, degrees in business and finance, and fifteen years of earlier experience in other kinds of financial institutions.

His most current specialty is "financial turnaround" in nonprofit health service organizations.

The challenge for the organization is to achieve a formal fiduciary status by getting out of a deficit that is threatening its existence. The personal challenge of the CFO is to reverse the tide for the organization by assuming fiduciary responsibility himself. That is a heavy load. Organizations that are in financial trouble hire such persons, he said, when they are losing money, cutting services, and often close to "getting out of the business."

School leaders do not typically work with deficits that may lead to "going out of business." Problems that many school leaders face involve providing better and more services than they are able to provide for the students with the limited funds that they have. Implementing educational mandates with insufficiently allocated external funds would be a better example. This interviewee does not possess financial powers related to programs, services, and clients. His powers are also limited. I hoped to learn about his work and the specialties that are required to assume fiduciary responsibilities under such conditions.

ACCOUNTING, AUDITING, BUDGETARY KNOWLEDGE, EFFICIENCY, AND REPORTING

At the outset of the interview I told the CFO that there is a debate in education as to whether or not, in hard financial times like these, school districts should be hiring financial specialists whose experience has not been in education. He said that he was not aware of this development. I also shared with him what I knew about the limited financial authority that school leaders have.

Author: As a CFO, are you personally liable for the organizational finances?

CFO: Yes. This means being responsible and legally liable for the financial operations of the institution.

Author: What are the fundamental skills that you possess that empower you to be liable?

CFO: Accounting and auditing.

Author: What does this actually mean?

CFO: This means keeping the accounts and examining them.

Author: Should school leaders possess these competencies, in your opinion?

CFO: Simple accounting and auditing skills are a must.

Author: What are other competencies that you use that you would consider basic ones?

CFO: It behooves you to know as much as possible about how budgets and finances actually work.

Author: Can you please elaborate?

CFO: Well, it is part of what the CFO needs to know. That includes what a budget is, an understanding of what I call the financial environments, and possible collaboration with other institutions may help, too.

Author: May I please ask you about the budgetary process itself? What actually goes on in the budgetary process in your institute? What is your involvement in it, and what kinds of knowledge and skills do you use?

The CFO first talked about how he and others work on making the annual projections of the organizational needs. In this rehabilitation center, the first budgetary consideration is that of the "maximum amount of deficit" that the center permits itself to face at the beginning of each coming year.

Author: Does that mean expecting a deficit, even planning for one?

CFO: Yes, these centers typically want to provide maximum amounts of services. They plan for corresponding incomes later. This involves projecting what services the center wants to provide, the amount of governmental and other income the center might receive for these services, and the difference between the two that the center assumes it can raise from private donors. This difference is decided first.

Author: Well, that is not how public schools work, although some schools are inevitably thrown into situations like this one at times of a crisis but not according to a plan.

CFO: The size of the deficit is determined each year by the board of directors of the center and by the chief executive officer (CEO). Once that decision is made, the CFO and eight additional members of what is called in the center "the professional leadership team" meet to project the volume of rehabilitation services that would be offered, the corresponding cost, the projected income, and a preliminary budget. The professional leadership team includes three vice presidents (for business development, fund development, and medical affairs) and five department directors (human resources, risk management, medical services, nursing, and rehabilitation services).

Author: You listed each group by starting with the administrative rather the medical areas.

CFO: I did, didn't I? The administrators in our institute are involved in the cost-benefits estimates.

Author: Does this group discuss income, too?

CFO: In our case, most donors sit on the board of directors. Board members know the rest of the donors personally.

I could not help but imagine how things might look if board of education members were also financial donors. In order to clarify for myself how the CFO sees relations between cost-benefit estimates and income, I asked if financial problems, or "deficits" as he calls them, are due primarily to inaccurately estimating the income from donors or to inaccurately estimating cost benefits.

CFO: Desired services are the benefits. Cost estimates of these benefits are done next. Some income is based on fees and contracts. Donations are added in next. And if you want to provide all the services, you figure out how much the deficit could be and how much more income from donations you would need.

Author: Please forgive me, but to me this sounds as somewhat irresponsible financial thinking.

CFO: Yes and no. If board members or other private donors do not cover the deficit, then this becomes irresponsible. But if the board guarantees to cover the deficit, then this is responsible.

Author: What else is important in what you call "budgetary knowledge"?

CFO: Well, we have not talked about expenditures.

Author: The CFO deals with twenty-five department heads, a number that is about the same as the number of teachers in some elementary schools.

CFO: My department heads are involved in cost-benefit estimation pretty much on the basis of my guidance. You might say that I lead this area and I coordinate it.

Author: Could you elaborate?

CFO: Simply put, I teach the middle management a thing or two about this part of the budgetary process. Together, we refine a proposed budget. This refers to adjusting the relationships between the desired services and how efficiently we could use the resources needed for them, all within the maximum deficit allowed by the board. Once this is done I go back to the CEO, and together we develop corresponding strategic goals. We also make needed changes in the organizational structure to suit revenue levels. This includes discount levels that the organization provides to nonagency payers as well as service levels, including contractual services that are provided with minimal expenditures.

Author: You mean structural changes are done before approved estimated incomes and approved expenditures are calculated and not the other way around?

CFO: Yes. The CEO makes the financial connections with the board on one hand and then with department heads on the other hand. I personally assume the lead role in these coordinating activities as well.

Author: And then?

CFO: Later in the budgetary process I become increasingly focused. I make recommendations that I believe are right. I validate the numbers associated with the estimated relationships of the benefits to the costs.

Author: [*I was wondering, what if leaders of large secondary schools made such proposals to the district administration?*]

CFO: I present my recommendations to the board's finance committee first and then to the whole board of directors. Board members ask questions during the meeting. I respond to the questions about various aspects of the recommended budget.

Author: What kinds of questions do they ask you?

CFO: The questions are typically about numbers, their meanings, services and activities, contracts, and other incomes.

Author: I am interested in learning more about the relations between the income with which you work, the internal allocations that are made, and the actual expenditures.

CFO: In my capacity as CFO I am intimately and completely familiar with all operational incomes except fundraising. I negotiate contracts and supervise their implementation from a financial perspective. I also control the flow of financial information.

Author: Does that mean that you are totally familiar with income sources and the terms under which the monies are received from each source?

CFO: I know the amounts in detail. Fundamentally, I am the person who creates the source of income through contracts. I must be familiar with it all.

Author: What about the fundraising? Why is your familiarity minimal?

CFO: If a categorical donation is made that requires a legal document, then I am involved. My role and expertise make me serve as the trustee of the gift. The gift itself becomes a beneficiary trust. When donors require no legal involvement on our part, I am not involved.

Author: [*We shifted gears.*] What kinds of instructions do you give to those twenty-five department heads when the monies are formally allocated to them, and in what kinds of financial monitoring are you involved?

CFO: All of the allocations that cover services are spelled out in the approved budget. Department heads have discretionary allocation powers within a ledger line item.

Author: Could you please give me an example?

CFO: The director of the physical therapy department receives a certain level of financial allocation for training. She decides how to spend it within the context of the spending policy. I sign off on the clinical policies.

Author: How does a finance person get involved in clinical policies?

CFO: As the CFO I have to write all the policies, with the exception of the charity care policies, as I told you before. These are more complex. I write all policies that involve federal regulations. I sign off on those that involve decisions by our director of admissions in individual areas.

Author: It seems that you are involved quite heavily in decisions associated with what services these departments will provide or perhaps even how. Am I right? How much do you know about the services themselves?

CFO: I am involved in almost everything regarding allocations and expenditures on a flow basis. I do not have to know the details of the services themselves.

Author: What about the board's involvement in allocation and expenditure decisions?

CFO: In the capital equipment expenditure there is usually a discretionary operating income associated with it. The fund is spent unless it is unavailable. In such cases the board approves the purchase, pending availability of the fund, and I sign off on it when it is actually spent.

Author: As you remember from our telephone conversation, school-leadership accountability is of interest to me.

CFO: You mean financial accountability?

Author: Well, for example, how do you make reports, and how do you demonstrate financial accountability? More specifically, sir, how do your financial statements look, and what is your involvement in preparing and presenting them? How do you project a sense of financial accountability? And what would you consider unethical reporting?

CFO: In the health systems, they are generations behind with regard to computer-generated financial reports. What I have to do is translate an Excel spreadsheet into a meaningful and flexible presentation of material that I prepare. Then I must verify that the information provided is "identical to reality." I review the information for accuracy. I usually request from department heads explanations for dollar amounts associated with services rendered. The sequence of my reporting goes like this: first to the CEO, then to the board's finance committee, and then to the whole board of directors.

My interviewee has actually developed a philosophy of financial accountability. He translates it into the report's ingredients as follows:

CFO: First, I believe that any reported comparisons must be objective and consistent.

Author: Could you please give me an example?

CFO: You cannot compare your first year to your predecessor's worst years. Whole periods are fairer. What you choose to compare to and what you choose not to compare to should be reasoned and clear.

Then he talked about information. He believes that only accurate information should be provided. If there are problems with inaccuracy or questionable accuracy, then it means that the report is not yet ready to be delivered. He also says that he must include in his financial reports information about why he has chosen to report what he did and also why he has chosen the reporting methods that he did.

The CFO had quite a bit to say about what he believed was unethical reporting. Below is his list, "regardless of the report's audience":

- An incomplete report
- A report that lacks thoroughness and accuracy
- A report that includes unaccounted-for items
- A report that includes actions that have not been insufficiently investigated
- A report that is modified to suit any particular person or group of people
- An incomprehensible report

I felt that this interview was helpful, and I thanked the CFO for his time. Then I asked him to identify competencies that he possesses and uses during the entire budgetary process, including the submission of his financial reports, that he believes school leaders could and should follow.

He first said that I had asked that before, and he had already answered. But then he continued by detailing the technical skills that are associated with accounting and auditing. Following that, he emphasized again the importance of understanding how finances operate in general as well as the exploration of joint ventures with others where the related financial considerations are central to the venture.

Author: Can you suggest examples about the last point?

CFO: Perhaps joint efforts among schools enable you to offer more courses or programs. It may increase efficiency. But I really do not know how much school leaders know about the finances of it. Perhaps they already know what they should know in this area. Not having a budgetary background is in and of itself a handicap. You need to recognize what you know and if and what more you need to know. Then you learn it. Maybe you need to ask your district to help you. Once educators know more about finances, they need to learn to listen to those who want things but who know less than they do about it. They have to control the language they use. They need to incorporate the financial aspects of ideas and convey them to others in a simple language. That is what happens to an educator who becomes a CFO, too, even without the title. This CFO is the one who is financially accountable.

Author: What if as a school leader you are accountable for so many other things, too, and you do not have much financial authority—I mean, are you not a CFO?

CFO: I have limited authorities. If a school has programs and personnel and clients and equipments and facilities and services, then there is also money involved. There is no way for the person who runs that school not to have some financial authority. That person must assume fiduciary responsibility regardless of the exact amount of financial authority she or he has. That person is the CFO.

9

Hospital Chaplain Provides Emotional Comfort

Hospitals wishing to provide spiritual care to their patients need to become accredited for this purpose. Once they become accredited, they may have volunteers performing this service, or they may have professional clergy, alone or with the assistance of a team of volunteers, providing such service. This service embodies providing comfort and solace to hospital patients and staff. It is a major challenge, and hospital clergy are specialists at how they face and meet it.

School leaders have a comparable challenge, listed sixth in this book. Some students, parents, teachers, and others in school will need comforting as they go through difficult times. There might be a physical injury, illness, or death. There are occurrences of detentions, suspensions, or expulsions. Students drop out. Students have to transfer to another school. There are times when violence, armed violence, and even arrest may occur. A hospital chaplain was interviewed in order to learn about specialties and accountability in providing emotional support.

The minister who was interviewed has been providing spiritual care in a hospital for eleven years, nine of them with the help of a team of volunteers that at the time of the interview numbered close to fifty members. This chaplain trains her volunteers before they begin to assist her in providing spiritual care to the hospital patients. She was fifty-two years of age when we talked. She possesses a BA degree in political science, an MA degree in curriculum and teaching, and another MA degree in divinity. She was formally trained as a chaplain, became board certified, and was ordained as a clinical pastoral educator. When you first see her, you realize how clearly she projects joyfulness about life itself.

Chapter 9

INTUITION, SPONTANEITY, AND COMMUNICATION

Author: In what way or in what ways, Reverend, do you view an illness or an injury that happens to a person?

Chaplain: Every traumatic event hurts, but it is also an opportunity. That is how I approach it. Even having your gallbladder taken out could be an opportunity for reflection, for a new thought, for change. A major catastrophe that involves death is an opportunity for the relatives for reflection as well.

Author: So it is the patient and those who are with the patient, not the injury or the illness, on which you focus. Am I right?

Chaplain: Yes. I see patients, their families, the hospital staff, the police at times, and others—all of them—in front of my eyes.

Author: What do you actually see?

Chaplain: I see people. Of course, I look at the medical, physical, and emotional status of the patient. But I see the person. It always depends on the multiple opportunities that exist for the patient and the loved ones.

Again "opportunities," I said to myself. How many of our school leaders would believe that a traumatic event in school is an opportunity? Opportunity for what, I asked myself. What opportunities could a school leader convey to a suspended student? Stay home and think about what you are missing? And what opportunities might a school leader talk about with a student who is severely injured because of armed violence in the school? Learn to defend yourself?

My mind swayed back and forth from seriousness to irony. The truth was that I had not (yet) fully appreciated the statement that the minister made: "Every traumatic event should be viewed as an opportunity."

Author: I hear you mentioning "opportunities." What do you mean by that, and why is it so important to you?

Chaplain: It is important to the patient and the loved ones. I look at the medical record and get a sense about it from the medical staff. I work from intuition about what I want to look at.

Author: What are you searching for?

Chaplain: The narrative is important to me.

Author: Is the narrative your guide?

Chaplain: Yes, my intuition informs me how to use the information in the narrative.

Author: [*What a principal knows about a student with problems would be important, I thought. But in an unexpected injury to a bystander, I did not have an equivalent.*]

Chaplain: These narratives guide me when I see the patient.

Author: When you go to provide comfort, do you have a plan?

Chaplain: No.

Author: But you spend time with the "narratives."

Chaplain: When I see the patient I act again from intuition. During our interaction I act mostly spontaneously.

Author: Is the use of intuition and your spontaneous behavior a requirement for being an effective provider of comfort?

Chaplain: Patients see intuitive and spontaneous behaviors as authentic. But I need to acquire information as a basis for these behaviors. That is why I consult first with the medical staff about the psychological status of patients.

Author: [*Earlier in her career she used to initiate most of the contacts that she had with the medical staff, but now the staff initiates the contacts as well.*] Why the change?

Chaplain: I guess the staff now better understands what we can do to help. They understand that ultimately our challenge is to provide comfort.

Author: Reverend, how do you communicate with a patient?

Chaplain: The first form of communication is being present there. While you are with the patient, you communicate as a function of what your intuition tells you to do.

Author: No rules?

Chaplain: Yes, there are restrictions. Also, I do not want to step on a land mine and have the patient become psychologically dependent on me.

Author: I understand.

Chaplain: You communicate in a spontaneous way. It depends on the patient and on what you know about the medical and psychological status of the patient. I now go not only to intensive care, cardiac care, and oncology but also to surgery. At times I want to know the inside of the body of the person to whom I provide solace. My general rule is, however, to get to know the patient no more than the patient wants me to know. The relationship develops intuitively, too, not just my part in the relationship.

Author: [*Such a relationship, I thought, might serve to neutralize adverse conditions of patients in a hospital. Could it and does it also serve this purpose in school, I wondered.*] Are you of the opinion, Reverend, that school leaders should strive to establish such relationships with those to whom they provide comfort?

Chaplain: Yes, I would. Providing comfort in ways that are not intuitive and spontaneous does not accomplish what it is intended to do.

Author: What about your communication competencies?

Chaplain: Providing comfort any place requires communication knowledge and skills that are very special. They include learning what difficult and uncomfortable situations call for and assessing the feedback or results. This includes listening, talking, touching, doing, and other things that are designed to provide emotional support to a person who strongly needs it. It also includes awareness of effects.

Author: To whom are you accountable, Reverend?

Chaplain: To my employer, but mainly to myself. No one sits with me and takes notes.

LOVE OF PEOPLE

My interest in the details intensified.

Author: Could you please give me an example of an interaction with a patient?

Chaplain: How a patient perceives my role affects the interaction greatly. For example, patients who have no spiritual faith tradition see me not necessarily as a spiritual caregiver at all. I must say that I learned that with time. At the beginning I used to approach my service to patients only from the spiritual sense.

She has only a few options at the beginning of the visit. She listens to the patient's narrative. At times she elicits a narrative. She listens as well as she can. Early in an interaction when she talks, say, with a cancer patient, she would typically not ask what the patient's job is but would rather say, "You have a full-time job to do, and that is to get well."

Chaplain: From that point on, many patients begin to actually reflect. They initiate these reflections themselves. The situations are fluid.

Author: What are the options?

Chaplain: The options for me become numerous. As far as I am concerned, the religious preference and discussions about it are way down the line. The narrative itself becomes the religious preference.

Author: I see.

Chaplain: The duration of the interaction is intuitively determined. I get clues from body language, eye contact, pain level, need for medication, and the presence or absence of medical staff.

Author: As patients reflect, what do they usually talk about?

Chaplain: They may provide an injury narrative or an illness narrative. They may talk about the present and/or about the past. They may talk about symptoms or about doctors. I once wanted to encourage an older patient to talk about other things as well, and I asked her what else happened in her life.

The patient answered that her husband had died a year and a half earlier and that only at that time had she realized that she had a serious kidney problem. I learned to be cautious here, yet I thought that it was good that the patient had sought help before it became too late and she was now talking about it.

Author: Can you share another example or two?

Chaplain: Some patients share relatives' stories or relationships stories. Older patients especially engage in that kind of narrative.

Author: Reverend, what would you say you provide most, psychological therapy, spiritual care, company, or other forms of emotional support?

Chaplain: I provide everything you mentioned, but the underlying common denominator is that I provide love.

Author: What kind of love?

Chaplain: The kind of love is not important as the love of what. I provide love of people. This is my specialty.

Author: How does it show?

Chaplain: Take the case in which a patient is dying. All people think of death. When you go under anesthesia you die for a while. All patients reflect upon death. It varies. People who are dying do it differently. My involvement must follow their wishes and attitudes, not precede them. The only way I can do it meaningfully is by loving people. At times, family members want me there. Some dying persons will say nothing. Others will just say, "I am dying."

At times, an attending physician opposes a family's request to be in the room. The physician feels that this is in the best interest of everyone. If the family insists, then the minister may intervene. When the family is in the room she may actually become quite involved. She would talk to family members, especially when they ask her questions. At other times when she is alone with the dying patient, she would respond to questions such as, "What is next for me?" or, "Is this the end of everything?" Her responses would depend on the way the dying patient perceives her role.

Author: Are there differences in your involvement with different families?

Chaplain: I let my love of people dictate what I do. When I am called in because of a cardiac arrest and sudden death, for example, I show my love to the deceased and to the members of the family. I talk to the family. I try to protect them from being exposed to intruding individuals. In traffic accidents, for example, the intruder might be a sheriff deputy. I feel empowered to shield the family who just suffered an abrupt loss of a dear one. In other situations, such as a lingering but fatal cancer, I show my love in becoming intimate with the family. The relationship would be a function of that family's wishes.

I asked her about her own feelings when she is involved in cases with a dying patient. At times, she intimated, she feels angry and frustrated. She feels so because she loves people and life. She is frustrated when a young person is dying ("has not lived long enough"), in a case related to drugs and alcohol ("brought it upon herself"), or when a driver takes all of the passengers with him or her to injury or death in an automobile accident ("not their fault at all"). "I am sorry, but I do not have pity or mercy," she says, "because we might all be there tomorrow." At other times the chaplain feels happy.

Author: How can you feel happy in times when you have to provide comfort?

Chaplain: If you love people and want the best for them, you certainly can and do feel happy. It happens, for example, when a very old person dies without pain and with the family right there. Once a nurse and I said to each other, "Wasn't that a beautiful, glorious death?"

Author: Do your spiritual-care team members also love people?

Chaplain: Each and every one of them does.

Most of the information about hospital patients is treated as confidential. Only a minimum amount of information about patients could be shared with the other members of this spiritual-care team. The chaplain selects the team members as carefully as a principal would select teachers. Team members in the hospital seem to easily learn about the different areas of medicine (hematology, oncology, etc.). The chaplain trains them. First, she appoints chaplain assistant coordinators, each one for a different religious faith. At present she has five chaplain assistants. Each one of these five recommends others from that religious faith, and she works with them, as well. School leaders who work with teachers at different grade levels in elementary schools might do the same. In high schools, the assistant principals and department heads are selected somewhat differently. The chaplain said, "The hardest thing to teach a team member is to know what to do with a particular kind of patient at any given time and how to do it well. I use the love of people as the bottom line."

Once she feels that she has helped instill self-confidence with a new volunteer, she makes the assignments with a view toward the best matches between individual members of each team and individual patients. One of this chaplain's assistants happens to be a retired priest and another is a psychologist. She uses their help in training team members.

Author: What is your view, Reverend, about love of people in schools and the role of the school leader in that? Is not love of people an inherent trait to some extent?

Chaplain: We are talking about providing emotional support and overall comfort. You could have a tragedy happening in school, God forbid. Bodily injury is not the only kind of injury. And some teenagers are expelled from school. Where can they go?

Author: Yes.

Chaplain: When you expel a student you have a psychological injury. To comfort requires love.

Author: Does loving make it easier to provide comfort?

Chaplain: I see it somewhat differently. When you love people, you want to help.

Author: Reverend, your challenges are so very meaningful. And I know that you meet them to the best of your ability. What does it take, the bottom line?

Chaplain: Good listening. Steering the discourses toward reflection, recovery, change, and the future. Caution. Spirituality. Shielding. Self-responsibility.

Author: What would you recommend to school leaders about providing comfort when needed in school?

Chaplain: All of the above and also what you asked me to talk about.

Author: What else?

Chaplain: I told you that I hold a teaching credential. Teachers, too, have to be intuitive and spontaneous. In elementary school, teachers provide comfort in that way all the time.

Author: Any other qualities or specialties school principals need to develop?

Chaplain: Oh, there is the obvious. You know, knowing your staff, your institution, your community, and also networking.

Author: If these were the obvious, what do you think is less obvious, that is unique to schools and school leaders when one thinks of providing comfort?

Chaplain: In order to provide comfort and support to people in need, you have to want to do it. I mentioned to you that I thought loving people makes you want to provide comfort when you see that it is needed. You have to like learning about a lot of things that matter to people. And teaching—you have to really like to teach. Teaching changes people's feeling—any place and at any time. Principals are in charge of teaching teachers in this regard, especially those who could use it.

Author: What are the required qualifications that one needs to pursue such challenges in school?

Chaplain: Each one of these things requires knowledge. You need to know yourself, too.

10

Courtroom Judge Manages and Adjudicates Conflicts

We are inching toward the completion of the report of the eight interviews. We need to examine searching two additional professionals and their challenges and two respective sets of specialized competencies that they use in meeting these challenges. School leaders could have much to learn from what a courtroom judge who manages and adjudicates conflicts and from a choral conductor who uses the chorus's performances as a beneficial teaching tool.

Conflict management and adjudication of a conflict in court is basically framing the conflict through judicious scrutiny into differences that may or may not be totally resolved. Seldom do both sides get everything they wanted. A judge is a constitutional officer, an elected or appointed public official, who is authorized to decide questions brought before the court. Backed by the law and authority, the judge is a specialist in managing and adjudicating conflicts.

There are municipal court judges, superior court judges, Supreme Court judges, judges who handle civil matters, and those who deal with criminal matters. I interviewed a superior court judge who handles civil matters. At the time of the interview the judge was fifty years of age and enjoying her job, although admitting to being bored sometimes. Her background includes a BA degree and a law degree, three- and ten-year tenures in two different district attorney offices, three months of service as a public defender, four years of service as a municipal court judge, and six years of service (as a governor's appointee) in her current position.

Author: Are you really bored at times?

Judge: It is recurring: the defendant or someone else testifies, and the lawyer does not get the point.

91

Author: Does the lawyer not "get the point" or does she not want to "get the point"?

Judge: Go on!

Author: So what do you do, Your Honor?

Judge: It is a matter of managing the case-managing time and managing the people.

Author: Do you have any personal problems with that?

Judge: I sit too long. I need to take care of my body. I need to be fresh and energized all the time.

Author: Well, I sure understand. Do you experience other specific problems?

Judge: When the lawyers argue, sometimes I get pain in my ear. Nothing serious. There are emotions at times, anger when someone lies or is not living up to their promises or expectations or showing disrespect toward the court. The best response is a gentle response.

Author: You experience lots of ills.

Judge: Go on.

In schools, I thought, the challenge of managing a conflict is usually less managing of lies and more managing opposing beliefs or opinions. Maybe the stakes are higher in court cases!

LEARNING ABOUT A CASE

Not every case goes to court. I was thinking of similarities in school where conflicts are often worked out informally and outside of the public eye.

Author: What does it take, Your Honor, to spare the system a court hearing?

Judge: It is a case-by-case situation.

Author: I mean with regard to your own involvement.

Judge: Well, this is a matter of learning the case, issues, sides involved, and potential outcomes.

Author: Can you please tell me more about how much you feel you need to know before getting involved in any given case?

Judge: I need to learn the case and as much as there is to know about what it involves.

Author: Well, would you recommend to a school principal to learn, as you do, about a case before getting involved in it?

Judge: Yes. But it depends on the available time, does it not?

A Superior Court has a civil division and a criminal division. This judge handles civil cases. The judges elect a president judge who assigns judges to one of the two divisions based on the personal experience and interest that each of the judges has. "The matches here are usually good," she said.

Within each division the cases are assigned at random. Her particular division handles 1,200 cases at any given time. But the status of each case is, of course, at a different stage. Scheduling the calendar of case hearings depends heavily on the legal limitation that a lawsuit must be filed within 120 days. About 90 percent of the case hearings must begin within a year of filing the case. The judge works simultaneously on several cases, at times up to hundreds of cases concurrently. The judge calls it "the river of justice flowing."

Judge: I complete seventy cases after climbing up to the top of the mountain. And then, you push them down, come down yourself, and seventy others are assigned to you. You study each one as much as you can. Some get settled outside of court. Others go to court.

Author: Do you ever excuse yourself from a case because of lack of authority?

Judge: No. It matters only if it is an issue of a relationship. It has to do with how close is one of the parties to anyone who sits on the adjudicating body. It is called "closeness." Look at what is happening now at the Supreme Court and the vice president of the United States.

Author: Who precisely is present with you in the courtroom, Your Honor?

Judge: First, there are two sides to the contention: the defendant and the defense attorney on the one hand and, of course, the prosecution on the other hand. Besides the judge you have the judge's staff, the jury, and court spectators. There are also situations in which one side may be filing a lawsuit against another. The plaintiff is the complaining party in the lawsuit. The defendant is the party that is required to provide answers in a legal action or suit. The lawyers engage in the acts of presenting the prosecution or the defense cases.

Author: When is a jury needed?

Judge: In court it is called "equity." Only a judge can handle the case in court. In what is called "law," the defendant has the right to a jury trial.

Author: [*I wanted to ask more about the jury, but she voluntarily started to talk about her staff.*]

Judge: My staff includes the bailiff, who deals with safety, security, and managing people; the clerk, who swears witnesses in and keeps records; and the court recorder, who puts the package of the proceedings together. Spectators are allowed in a public trial. They must not interrupt.

Author: What about the media?

Judge: In the O. J. Simpson trial it got out of control. It was a show, a performance. Perceptions replaced facts frequently. It became impossible. In my court you might occasionally see a newspaper reporter who takes notes or a still cameraperson if the lawyers agree—no television cameras of any sort. The lawyers in my court have never agreed to that. I am on the conservative side myself, as well.

Author: Why?

Judge: I am not sure about reporters. Last week one came, sat here, wrote some notes for five minutes, and left.

The judge was wondering what this reporter saw and could understand about the case by being present in the courtroom for just five minutes. Yet the next day there was a whole article in the newspaper about it. She wants to minimize such developments. She cannot be responsible for them. As to a click of a still camera, it is bothersome to her. There is no need to take more than one picture. "Jurors," she said, "must not be photographed anyway."

AMICABLE MEANS

When serious conflicts occur in school, the media is often there. Not only do school leaders need to handle the conflict itself in the best way that they can, but they also have to handle the media. Caution and prevention, I thought, is what the judge exercises. I asked her about it.

Judge: Yes, you might say so. My goals here are focused on the case and avoiding a show. I am also a strong advocate of presiding over a court proceeding using the most amicable means. That is what the public expects from a judge.

Author: What does that mean, Your Honor?

Judge: I guide, perhaps teach at times, the jury. I make procedural rulings. When there is no jury I evaluate the evidence and decide the case myself. When there is a jury, its members are the judges, and I tell them so. But I still have to know everything that there is to know about the case. Yet I must remain neutral insofar as evaluating the evidence.

Author: How easy or difficult is it to do, I mean being amicable and being neutral?

Judge: The process has to be fair and peaceful. When there is a jury, I am less involved with the content. I feel less responsible for the outcome. I do not decide the case. A major challenging phenomenon in a court situation is that the defendant is considered innocent until proven guilty.

Author: [*The judge dwelled on the fact that judgments ought not to be made in advance.*]

Judge: Another major challenging phenomenon in court is that the prosecution typically hammers at the defense. A skillful lawyer appears confident. Law is persuasion. The jury may not see everything. I must be in charge of the rulings in relation to the objectives of what is said in court. I must also explain to the jury when necessary the meanings of what is heard and what is occurring in court. What we got from England is a system of law that involves fairness in treatment and remediation in justice, and these are the guidelines I communicate to the jury.

Author: [*For a moment I thought about a jury or an advisory committee or even a few people to consult with when managing and adjudicating a conflict in school.*] Please, teach me more about jurors, Your Honor.

Judge: For an accused party to have a jury is a right, a given and an undisputed right.

Author: Does everyone who might be a potential juror know this?

Judge: Potential jurors do not necessarily pay that much attention to this. To some people this is not a sufficient reason to want to serve as jurors. To others, it is even a nuisance. I try to persuade people that this duty is crucial to the existence and to the effectiveness of the legal system. If and once they are chosen, they possess judicial authority. I tell them that. It allows me to be more fair myself.

Author: Their identity is confidential until the end of the case.

Judge: Yes.

Author: Does the presence of a jury contribute to fairness?

Judge: Its presence is a right.

Author: What do you consider fair, and what do you consider unfair?

Judge: Credibility of the evidence is a problem. Questions at times are not sufficiently specific. There needs to be a time limit on questioning. Motions for mistrial are a right even if it consumes more time and other resources. I follow up on everything that I find is justified, even if it creates a problem. I alone evaluate the evidence in a motion for mistrial. Despite the fact that the law today is decreasingly formal, rules are still followed. Courtroom proceedings have an enormous influence on what the outcome will be.

Author: Even if hearings of cases related to conflicts in schools are not courtrooms, would you recommend to principals to be involved in formal fact-finding?

Judge: It looks better if fact finding is a formal process. It contributes to fairness without losing amicability.

Author: About requests for "mistrials," should schools allow them? I am thinking, for example, of a parent or a student who comes to the principal challenging a ruling made by a teacher or by an assistant principal—or someone going to the district superintendent challenging a ruling that a school principal made.

Judge: By now you realize that I do not recommend much to others, other than being fair and behaving amicably.

MODEL BEHAVIORS

Author: May I ask a few questions about your own behavior, Your Honor, as you manage and adjudicate conflicts in court?

Judge: Are you asking about routine procedures?

Author: You have helped me understand those quite well. I am also interested in what you do and how you do it, the form, the tone, the intermediate goals, particularly when problems persist.

Judge: If you mean in relation to problems in court, then come and see. I try to behave not only appropriately but also for others to see and do the same. If you mean contentious situations in general that are brought before the courts of law, then I told you that the public expects the court to manage and resolve these situations amicably, peacefully.

Author: Yes, Your Honor. Anything else that is important for me to know about how you do what you do?

Judge: The public has expectations from the court's behavior. What could make it easier to work peacefully with all parties is to systematically transform the conflict into problems and then work on them. How else can the public have trust in the judiciary?

Author: You focus on the public, Your Honor. Should public school leaders, in your opinion, also consider what the public expects in situations involving conflicts?

Judge: What are the kinds of laws that back up school principals in such cases?

Author: [*I tried another approach.*] Which particular competencies might you employ in court other than those related directly to the law?

Judge: With my staff, it is teamwork. With lawyers, it is leading by example. With the jury, it is teaching.

Author: [*I asked her to elaborate.*]

Judge: Everyone is a human being. But relationships depend on people's role in court. The staff starts and ends together. Each person knows what his or her role is during and following the court proceedings. That is why we are a team.

Author: So you are a member of this team?

Judge: Yes.

Author: What about the lawyers?

Judge: The lawyers have vested interests. Their behaviors go together with their arguing skills. They push in certain directions that they think would benefit their causes. What they say may be true. Here I have to lead by example, to cut them off if needed, but to show what I think is relevant. You have to move things along and in an appropriate manner.

Author: Is it difficult to do?

Judge: Call it model behavior on my part.

Author: What about the jury?

Judge: About the jury, it consists of lay individuals. The jury is also a team. Teaching them the law and the proceedings is of the essence.

Author: Do you serve as a teacher to both the jury and the lawyers if you can?

Judge: Call it model teaching.

Author: In order to serve as a model teacher, what special competencies do you have that enable you to do it?

Judge: I do not need special competencies. I need to know no more than what is known to me. How I share what I know is critical. The lawyers watch each other. They do most of the finding out. They also resist revealing some things. Model teaching is doing what needs to be done, emphasizing that you are doing what needs to be done, and that you expect the same from others. It is leading by example.

Author: [*I thought of the contending parties involved in a conflict in school.*] Would you please elaborate a bit further on the notion of leading by example insofar as the lawyers in the courtroom are concerned?

Judge: As I said, people expect that courts will resolve conflicts peacefully. This implies that I expect the lawyers to respect the court. It is my job to control them, if necessary. I respect the lawyers as well, of course. I respect everyone else in my court.

Author: Anyone else?

Judge: I highly value my staff and the services that they provide to the court, especially when they make my court appear effective. I motivate and inspire them.

The key remaining issue for me at that point was to clearly identify her philosophy and competencies that might be relevant to school leaders as they face the challenge of trying to handle contentious conflicts. I was left with the need for confirming specifics. With extreme caution I enumerated briefly to the judge some of her statements that I had heard and others that I had inferred:

- becoming acquainted first, learning what you should and could about the case first;
- turning a conflict fairly and amicably into issues that have to be solved; and
- behaving as a model for others while managing procedures and adjudicating.

Here is what the judge answered.

Judge: I know that school leaders face major challenges today. If there is anything that I mentioned that turns out to be useful to them, then I would be happy to know that it did.

Author: May I list these three recommendations for them, Your Honor, and ask them how helpful they are to them?

Judge: You certainly may.

11

Choral Conductor Makes Beneficial Uses of Performances

I must admit that originally I knew of and used the term "choir" rather than "chorus." My eighth and last interviewee taught me that "choir" generally refers to a religious organization and "chorus" can be part of an opera, a school, a community group, and so forth. The quality of the singing may be the same in both the choir and the chorus. Teaching to perform and directing a performance may be the same in both situations. But the kinds of uses that a conductor might be making of the actual performing achievement of the singers may not be the same.

A chorus conductor teaches the musical pieces to the chorus, directs it, and uses the actual performances of the chorus in beneficial ways. The conductor is a specialist who devotes a large portion of her or his time to prepare for each concert but also for activities following each concert.

In my interview of such a specialist, I was hoping to learn about all of those activities, their specific purposes, the specialties needed to engage in them, and about their relationship to the conductor's views about accountability. The school leaders' pursuit of our eighth and last challenge involves comparable activities as well.

Our thirty-nine-year-old interviewee has attained a BA, an MA, and a doctoral degree in the area of music. He serves as artist in residence in an academy that is a specialized secondary school for the performing arts in a large unified school district. He has previously done similar work in two small liberal arts colleges and in another secondary school, a magnet high school for the performing arts. He says that he is very happy being involved in this kind of work.

This interview was quite structured because, during the preliminary discussions with him, I had felt that a structured interview would be appropriate in this case. He just seemed to be a highly logical type of person. I asked the chorus conductor several sets of questions that relate to his overall work, beginning with the following:

Author: When a decision is made to develop and maintain an ongoing chorus in an educational organization, what do you believe are the anticipated expectations that the organization has for this chorus?

Conductor: Ideally, the dual purpose includes educating students and entertaining audiences. I have found out that educating audiences about choral music literature is essential as well.

Author: Maestro, could you please elaborate on this last point?

Conductor: The chorus offers performances to different audiences. As a learning unit and a concert performer, the chorus presents high-quality music at a professional level. The chorus is also an ambassador of the school. It can help persuade prospective students to enroll and prospective donors to write checks. In some schools, the chorus can also serve as an alternative program option for troubled students.

How many school leaders, I thought, would be courageous enough to replace "student achievement" in each of the statements here for the term "student concert"?

I asked him to continue dealing with the expectations in a bit of detail. According to him, the first piece of detail is that, once a decision to have a chorus is made in a school setting, (1) a qualified "musician and leader," is hired and (2) sufficient financial support, "for both technical and managerial functions" is secured. Typically, a single individual would be taking on the roles of "teacher, director, and conductor." In addition, a system is established whereby members of the ensemble are selected. For a given year, the literature to be performed is selected as well as the nature and venues of performances.

PRAISE AND STRENGTHENING THE SENSE OF OWNERSHIP

Author: Who are the audiences when the chorus performs?

Conductor: A variety of them: students, parents, the school district administration, and the community are the most common audiences. A balance has to be established between what kind of musical literature the chorus conductor wants the chorus to learn to sing and perform and what audiences seem to prefer. Also, a balance has to be achieved between what each of these audiences wants. The pieces that the director chooses are central. The director represents the music and the musicians.

He further explained that audiences actually range from those who attend public performances to those who sponsor or attend private engagements. As a school ambassador, the chorus might perform for an audience that may include prospective donors and prospective students. Other schools' musicians can be audiences as well. This happens when the chorus is on a tour. There are music-exchange trips, as well.

Author: So, you see the audiences as also being promoters, sort of stakeholders of the chorus?

Conductor: Stakeholders or those whom I would like to have become stakeholders.

Author: Why are they important to you?

Conductor: I mentioned to you some reasons and examples, but I want to have as wide a set of people as possible interested in what we do.

Author: You mentioned sponsors, prospective donors, potential singers, and the school as a whole, and you mentioned the role of general ambassadorship.

Conductor: You need all these audiences in order to expand the ownership, not of the chorus (I am the director), but of the beautiful music that we perform.

Author: Is that why you interact with the audience during concerts? I saw you a couple of times, and you seem to be part of the performance.

Conductor: I announce but also teach. It is an emcee function. Interpreting music for the audience and even acting with a tinge of humor are important functions. That helps to bring the audience to the music and how it is performed. It is a service.

Author: Maestro, you work in a school. Would you recommend that a school principal also engage in these kinds of "stage activities"—I mean, in relation to student achievement on tests, for example?

Conductor: I really would not know. I suppose the principal might explain test scores to people, praise the students, and have people feel that they are part of the achievement.

Author: How?

Conductor: Well, you need to understand what the scores mean, and you need to explain with enthusiasm, charisma, and praise of what has been achieved.

Author: Are there ways to prepare for such activities?

Conductor: We do it continuously, all year long, not just after a major concert. Think of new students, funds, publicity, exposure, and at times, also an opportunity to perform for any group, such as another school, a particular musical work before it is presented to the public at large or before it is presented in a competition.

Author: Interschool comradeship, so to speak?

Conductor: Yes, both in preparation for a competition and during a competition. On such tours, musicians exchange music and e-mail addresses for correspondence about a variety of performances. This expands the musicians' world.

Author: As you know, sir, principals do not select students nor do they teach students directly. So their influence on the way the music is played in the concert—that is, scores on standardized tests—is at best chancy and indirect.

Conductor: You work with what you have. I do, too.

Author: Just a few questions about singers, please.

- What do you actually do when you audition them for the chorus?
- What do you look for?
- And how do you make your final choices of singers?

And here are some more questions.

- What are the things that you do when you teach the singers to sing as a chorus?
- What do you look for when you examine possible music to use in performances?
- And how do you make your final choices of music for a given performance?

Conductor: [*He began patiently.*] Each auditioning student is allotted fifteen minutes to complete the audition requirements. After having completed a written application with supporting materials, they are given a time slot on the day of audition. During that time they are in the choral room with a panel of adjudicators who advise the director, and the accompanist, if requested.

Author: What do you look for?

Conductor: The audition process determines whether one has sufficient talent or potential, as well as a good attitude and work ethic. Singers are asked to perform a prepared song. Then, they are checked for range, ability to match and remember pitches and pitch patterns, asked to sing a scale a cappella, and given an opportunity to learn a new excerpt of music. A short set of questions is also part of the process. These questions help determine the level of the fit.

ANALYSES FOR IMPROVEMENT

Author: When you say "fit," Maestro, you mean the particular role of a singer in the chorus?

Conductor: While taking into consideration the needs of the school and the department of musical arts, the decision of admission is based on whether by talent or by potential the student will be able to succeed in the program. Sometimes we need to look at a certain part of the audition over again before a final admission can be made. Sometimes even a major deficiency will not stop the person from being accepted, whereas a slight problem with another student may result in rejection. This is a case-by-case process, but the decisions are always the director's, without any pressure from others. Lobbying is okay.

Author: [*My mind shifted from inability to select who attends a school in our case to the curricular requirements that school districts give to schools.*] What about the music, Maestro?

Conductor: It is music and more. The major curriculum points can be found on the website at www.sfsota.org (click on "The Arts at SOTA" and "Vocal"). Our curriculum includes character development through individual and social responsibility skills, music theory and composition, sight singing, vocal production, large and small choral works spanning seven hundred years, small art songs in many languages, barbershop quartets to jazz singers, leadership, and community service. Personally, I am a choral director, a teacher, a conductor, an actor, a manager, a coach, a cheerleader, and a therapist.

Author: What about talking with the singers after a performance? Do you hold a postbriefing session afterward?

Conductor: Oh yes, but I do it in steps with them and without them.

Author: Could you please elaborate?

Conductor: Basically, it includes immediate praise and an informal chat right after the concert, occasional unplanned chats later with individual singers, and then comes the summer.

Author: What happens in the summer?

Conductor: Most of the work related to analysis of the year, its successes and happenings, I do in the summer. This work is the basis for the coming year. I select music and performance dates and venues. I also plan collaborative works, such as a major work for chorus and orchestra. This kind of work requires attention to detail, ranging from distribution of music to rehearsal and performance coordination.

During the summer this conductor plans the music just for his major concerts. This music revolves around themes (seasonal or specific event). It may also be a presentation of one or more composers, languages, styles, genres, and so on. The conductor described to me several ways in which he could organize programs. He suggested that one could combine them while still being thorough in one's survey of the music.

Some of the music is planned during the school year. Additional music may be learned for specific events throughout the academic year. Such events might even include a funeral or a school board inauguration.

Author: Could we please go back to the "fit"? Is it between a singer and a role?

Conductor: One cannot reasonably perform music written for sopranos, altos, tenors, and basses if three-quarters of the chorus are men. Also, it is not reasonable to expect every person to perform all music. Advanced groups can be created, depending on the need. They can meet at a separate time and rehearse other music. Opportunities are available for people who want to sing in the community. Music is selected accordingly.

Author: [*There is relevance from his search for "fit," I thought, to what principals might do with test results. Perhaps analyzing achievement test results and dissecting concert performances might be comparable. But principals do not choose the tests!*] What about your final selections for a given performance?

Conductor: It all is a function of the vision of the program and the specific performances, all of them. It is the conductor's responsibility to visualize and carry it all out. Students should learn, and the audience should hear at least one major choral/instrumental work and at least two extended choral works with instruments and/or soloists.

Author: Is it solely your decision to work with these requirements in mind?

Conductor: Yes. There is content that needs to be covered for a round of choral education, and there are standards of performances, too.

Author: [*Sounded familiar: domain and standardized achievement tests.*] Are your rehearsals designed in relation to respective concerts?

Conductor: Yes.

Author: [*I was thinking now of preparations for achievement tests.*] Allow me, Maestro, to pose the following questions about rehearsals:

- To what extent is your instruction during rehearsals a function of the analyses that you made in the summer?
- Do you provide individual instruction?
- What do singers need to do between rehearsals?
- And to what extent do you change activities from rehearsal to rehearsal, and what might be some of the changes?

The conductor's comments on these topics were extensive. First, he expects singers between rehearsals to maintain good physical and mental health. He also wants them to learn the required music quickly and accurately, as well as to complete all the assigned work on time. He draws up a contract with the students. They sign it. He expects them to honor it, including their promise of "a positive demeanor conduct."

When he works with individual singers or groups of singers, he provides lessons that include texts, notes, rhythms, articulation, dynamics, general interpretation, and vocal instructions. This depends on the "learning point of the music," as he calls it. He says that items addressed in choral settings typically include balance, blend, diction, dynamics, interpretation, intonation, and precision.

As to rehearsals, they vary depending upon the time of the year and the proximity to a concert. As part of his "gestalt" (as he calls his total challenge to put out the best performances that he can), he does several things during rehearsals:

- He introduces new members to the group.
- He has singers read new music.
- He leads discussions regarding philosophy and protocol.
- He reviews the elements of vocal production or music theory.
- He has the singers work on specific chords or phrases.
- He discusses meanings of texts.
- He reviews the needs of an upcoming performance.
- And he discusses a recent event or performance.

The conductor found it difficult to answer the question about possible changes from rehearsal to rehearsal because, as he said, "so many situations come up. One can always plan the big picture. But the daily plan and what/how you say and do things in rehearsals are often dictated by what happened yesterday and what you think the reaction will be tomorrow. It is a constant balancing act."

His answer to the question about the uniqueness of the general rehearsal was this:

Conductor: I am pretty good at knowing the music and knowing the people. I can identify problems and solve them. I make sure to structure the general rehearsal so that people will leave with the feeling that they have accomplished good things, made good music, become better musicians, and enjoyed themselves.

Author: This perplexes me. Did you mean that, given your singers and their ability, you know what the actual performance will look like and that the general rehearsal is actually perfunctory?

Conductor: Certainly it was not proofreading. An unexpected error may show up in the concert itself, too.

Author: How about the goals of solidifying social cohesion of the chorus members or intensifying the support that one singer might give to another?

Conductor: That is important.

Author: What are the things that you do or do not do before, during, and after a performance, in comparison to the general rehearsal?

I followed up on this question by asking if he, in fact, seeks critiques of a given performance and, if so, what he looks for in those critiques.

The conductor divided his responses into what happens during a performance and what happens following a performance. In the first case, he said, it is important to help keep the focus and the confidence of the singers. It is also extremely important to help them be what he calls "vocally prepared." And then he added the following:

Conductor: One can only encourage and instruct concerning immediate logistics. Philosophy and long-term music-learning techniques will not help the pitch get ten more cycles per second sharper. Those unfixable things and any errors need to be let go of at the time. The sooner the error is forgotten, the better the chance of a smoother duration of the performance. Some people turn off lights or have singers hold hands or close eyes before going on stage, encouraging group focus and unity.

Author: So identifying in the general rehearsal what to improve for the actual performance should have boundaries?

Conductor: Yes, but if you feel that the singers need to be aware of certain things following the concert, you convene them for a short lesson, not just a chat.

Author: What would you do?

Conductor: I would address every relevant issue. The issues I would discuss would range from music to logistics. Someone always has a funny story, and we can always find something around which to rally for improved future performance.

As the interview progressed it became fully clear how directly the chorus conductor is able to work toward enhancing the quality of the performances of chorus singers in concerts. School principals are not in such a direct position to influence the quality of the scores that students attain. Teachers are in a more direct position.

Author: Maestro, do you believe that principals could help teachers improve student achievement in the same way that you do when you reflect on deficiencies in performances?

Conductor: I am not familiar with the details about the nature and extent to which principals and teachers interact with regard to test scores.

Author: Should they?

Conductor: I suppose so. Information about performance scores should be used for improvement.

Author: Might I suggest, Maestro, that student performance on an achievement test is scored individually. A mean score may be computed for a class, a grade level, or a school. The performance of the chorus is a group performance. It is not an overall of scores on a test that individual students take. It is a single phenomenon that cannot be dissected in different ways. A concert could go sour because of one singer. The mean score on a test taken by several students in a school would not be drastically changed by a score of one individual.

Conductor: Well, yes, these are different situations.

Author: Despite the differences, do you have any specific suggestions to principals and teachers about using achievement data for improvement?

Conductor: What about together analyzing the achievement, the performance on the tests, and then coming up with changes in the grouping, the teaching, whatever.

Author: What do think it would take?

Conductor: First you want to want to do it and, [*second,*] knowing the "singers and the music" [*is important*]—I mean the students, the curriculum, and the performance.

Author: Were you trained in analyzing performances for improvement purposes?

Conductor: I taught myself.

Author: How important is it, then, to become a specialist in analyzing the performance for improvement purposes?

Conductor: In my work it is part of the job. It is my responsibility.

Author: What else, Maestro, can I learn from you?

Conductor: Good chorus conductors and good school principals should be aware of everything that could improve learning, including operating policies and their execution. Greater goals of the institution, the bigger picture, and the ways to achieve the greater goals are also important. Ability to organize and manage with charisma helps to arrange for good uses of student achievement information.

Author: What about interaction with the teachers, Maestro?

Conductor: I think that often school principals need to be more aware of the daily challenges facing their staff. While worrying about the overall picture, school leaders sometimes do not fully understand the scope and background of the needs that face them. Instructors are often left to accept situations that are inconvenient or awkward. Good communication between teachers and administrators is critical to a positive, healthy, and productive educational working environment.

Without a doubt, here he spoke as a knowledgeable teacher.

III

SURVEYING SCHOOL LEADERS

12

Specialists Recommend Special Competencies

Eight challenges that school leaders face were originally conceived. Eight professionals in fields other than school leadership offered respectively to school leaders recommendations about the pursuit of each challenge. We wanted to do a validity check of the challenges and the recommendations made by the external specialists.

Therefore, each recommendation was rewritten in a direct way rather than as an implied one. We also used language that related to the improvement of the effectiveness in meeting the challenge. An attempt was made to have the language "school leader friendly." Ultimately, we selected from the interviews twenty-four recommendations that are described below, along with the rationale for each one that we deduced from the specialists making the recommendations.

THE AIRLINE CAPTAIN'S FIVE RECOMMENDATIONS FOR ACHIEVING PREDETERMINED GOALS

School principals should have served first as assistant principals. The airline captain must serve first as a copilot. A copilot gains first-hand experience in communicating with the passengers and the tower and with flying the aircraft above ten thousand feet. The captain sees the assistant principal position as constituting equivalent experience in school.

School leaders should hold staff meetings whenever someone new comes on board. Seldom does the airline captain fly with exactly the same crew. So prior to each flight, the captain familiarizes the copilot, the A line, and the rest of the crew with his expectations, particularly in cases of emergency.

The captain sees the need in school to act as a team in which each member knows what to expect from the principal and from each other.

School leaders should assume responsibility for problems before they communicate them to others. With regard to assuming responsibility for problems that occur that need to be communicated to followers, the captain believes that every leader should do so. This needs to happen because that is what leaders must do in times of trouble. Communicating about a problem without having first taken responsibility for it, in his mind, leaves the followers' sense of confidence at a low level.

School leaders should prioritize their objectives in times of serious problems as follows: safety, comfort, schedule, and efficiency. In the air, safety is the most important concern of aircraft leaders. The same holds for schools. Without safety, nothing good can proceed. The captain's concern with comfort reflects his assumption that without comfort, it is difficult to function. Arriving on time at a predetermined destination is important in his mind but not at the expense of safety and comfort.

His attitude toward the instruction and learning schedules is probably the same: important but only after safety and comfort are assured. Even if he needs to use an extra amount of fuel in order to preserve safety and comfort, he stays in the air until it is safe to land. He sees the extra cost to his company as a must in such situations but only up to a point. Efficiency is still an objective for him. He would like to see the same kind of thinking occurring in schools.

School leaders should be screened for autonomy to make decisions and to act. To the best of our knowledge this practice is not common in school leadership. One reason, perhaps, is the perception of interviewers who choose principals that principals have to show ability to follow school district policies as well as involve their staffs in decision making in the school. A high score on either one of these measures does not necessarily reflect principal autonomy. It may even reflect the opposite—low principal autonomy.

The captain in his cockpit must make final decisions independently of the tower and the passengers. He wants school leaders to do the same. He wants them to be selected for autonomy because he feels that they often need to act independently of the desires of school district and the teachers in the school.

THE POLICE OFFICER'S SIX RECOMMENDATIONS FOR MAINTAINING SAFETY AND ENFORCING THE LAW

School leaders should spend as much time as possible being visible in potentially problematic areas. Situations that are potentially unsafe or that lend themselves to violating the law are continuously on the policeman's mind. He recommends the same to school leaders if safety is to be maximized and the law is to be enforced in school. Being visible in places where individuals are most likely to become unsafe or break the law might prevent or at least reduce such incidences.

School leaders should be comfortable acting from a position of authority. The policeman speaks here about authority that reflects formal empowerment to do what he does. He believes that without it he could not accomplish what he has to do. He also knows that, at times, individuals who need to do what is unpleasant to others (ticket for speeding, arrest for a crime) may feel uncomfortable doing it. Since acting from authority enhances what they need to do, they must become comfortable with doing so. The law-enforcement officer feels that the same should happen in schools. School leaders should be comfortable acting from authority to do what is unpleasant to others, such as imposing detention and suspension.

School leaders should work toward maximizing cooperation and collaboration with other individuals and agencies in order to eliminate confusion. In problematic situations that the police officer faces, this is what he has to do. Medical personnel, firefighting personnel, and officials from other agencies may be called to the scene of an accident. Cooperation and minimum confusion are needed in order to save lives and property and in order to enhance the investigation of wrongdoing if there is any. The officer sees law enforcement and medical personnel needing to work together in the same manner with school leaders when necessary.

School leaders should help teachers act from a position of authority. Just like a law-enforcement officer on the road helps others who are there to feel comfortable acting from a position of authority, so should leaders in school. Teachers or other staff members (such as assistant principals facing bullying behavior or violence) should act immediately and do so from a position of authority. The police officer believes that especially in schools, where staff members do not wear official uniforms, helping staff to act from a position of authority is essential.

In the event that a law-enforcement person is on the school campus, school leaders should become fully aware of what is occurring, the related law, and the consequences. If accepted and implemented, this recommendation would help the officer if he has to be on the school grounds. That is probably the major reason for him making this recommendation.

School leaders should be able to easily interpret districtwide rules for student behavior and promptly apply them in order to avoid confusion. The officer must follow such requirements himself when he detects a driver breaking the law. With this recommendation, the officer is implying that, perhaps, as it is on the road, difficulties in interpreting laws and rules in schools could lead to, among other problems, confusion. Confronting confusion about interpreting the law on the road is embarrassing and makes the enforcement of the law difficult. The officer probably feels that the same pitfall should be identified and minimized in schools.

THE CROP GROWER'S TWO RECOMMENDATIONS FOR ENHANCING STUDENT BENEFITS

School leaders should consider schoolwide learning and growth problems as interference and act to minimize them decisively, authoritatively, and efficiently. This is exactly what happens in crop growing. The grower sees any problem with the crop as interfering with crop growth. That is why he sees any problem with learning and teaching as interference with student growth. He also sees the need to minimize the interference in crop growing decisively, authoritatively, and efficiently. To him, in the business of crop growth, someone with authority must decide on what to do in order to minimize inefficiency in the growth. He feels that the same should be done with reducing interference (problems) with student growth in school.

School leaders should prepare the school experiences in tune with ultimate job and higher education opportunities, including offering fundamental and specialized curricula and benchmarks and exit tests. The crops that the grower grows are sold for profit. The best that can happen to school graduates, in his opinion, is getting a job or enrolling in an institution of higher education. For the grower, the outcome is the key, both in the field and in school. During the process of growing crops the grower performs fundamental duties. He feels that the equivalent is needed in the enforcement of the curricula that the school offers. He specializes in crop growing and, therefore, also in what it takes to do so objectively. That is how he views the principal and the curriculum.

THE AUTOMOBILE SERVICE ADVISOR'S THREE RECOMMENDATIONS FOR HELPING TO SOLVE PROBLEMS

School leaders should reflect on the decisions they make in terms of what and how to communicate them. In the automobile repair business, service advisors know that customers typically come in with a problem vehicle. The problem causes inconvenience. Fixing the problem costs money. Few people come in happy to the garage. Customers are often vulnerable. They have to listen to what has to be done to their cars. What they hear should be planned in advance. That is the service advisor's message.

It is he who needs to communicate to the customer about what is wrong, what might be done, how long it will take, and how much it might cost. He has to communicate in the best possible way. It is probably this picture that is in front of the service advisor's eyes when he thinks about principals who are confronted with people who come to them with problems of all sorts. How the problem and the solution are communicated is critical to the advisor.

School leaders should improve their ability to market the school. The service advisor sees the school as providing a service. Just like any other service, including what he provides, he sees it as in need of being marketed. He thinks that school leaders do not do enough of this.

School leaders should make decisions more from the heart than they do now. In his business, the decisions are highly rational and based mainly on facts. Any one of the repair recommendations that he makes will cost money. To him, one must be sensitive to that and feel empathy for the customer. Problems are costly in schools, too. He feels that school leaders often do not express sufficient empathy when they make decisions that are costly to students (zero tolerance, suspension, expulsion).

THE CHIEF FINANCIAL OFFICER'S RECOMMENDATION FOR ASSUMING FIDUCIARY RESPONSIBILITY

School leaders should acquire budgetary knowledge over and above simple accounting and auditing, including learning how budgets operate, their contexts, and with consideration of the need to increase efficiency. These are the functions the CFO in the nonprofit medical rehabilitation service performs. He feels that despite the fact that a great portion of the financial authority in education is not vested in the school itself, the school principal should learn to engage in similar functions to those that he (the CFO) does.

His reasons might be anchored in the need to describe and interpret financial conditions to different stakeholders, the need to raise funds from private sources, and the need to identify the public financial resources to which special applications for special grants might be made. The CFO also thinks of the need to make financial projections into the future in both his and the school organizations.

THE HOSPITAL CHAPLAIN'S TWO RECOMMENDATIONS FOR PROVIDING COMFORT

School leaders should improve their intuitive, spontaneous, and communicative skills. The chaplain sees sickness, injuries, and death. She sees people suffering and their loved ones suffering. Each person is different. Each moment may be different. The chaplain sees many difficult situations during a given unit of time. To provide spiritual care and comfort in such situations requires much more than just knowledge. The chaplain believes that intuitiveness and spontaneity reflect authenticity. She knows that there are injuries and punishments in schools and that comfort can relieve psychological pain.

In order to provide solace when needed, school leaders should love people, learning, and teaching. She cannot provide solace without loving people because solace is based on loving another person. In order to provide solace she must learn about whom she is providing solace. And in order to provide solace she needs to know how people can learn to accept it. According to her, the desire to know and learn grows with increasing love. These might be her reasons for this recommendation.

THE COURTROOM JUDGE'S THREE RECOMMENDATIONS FOR MANAGING AND ADJUDICATING CONFLICTS

School leaders should learn about a conflict before getting involved. Courtroom judges who are assigned to cases must try to study each case thoroughly before it goes to court. At times, because of this extensive study the judge is able to convince the two sides to settle their differences out of court. If the case goes to court the judge manages the court proceedings with legal authority and personal touches. The judge we interviewed saw the resolution, and even the management of conflicts without a resolution, in school needing to be the same in principle. Her reasons are probably more related to her use of conflict-resolution and conflict-management skills than to the fact that the law backs her up.

School leaders should turn conflicts and confrontations into problems to be solved by amicable means. The courtroom judge sees each case as a conflict between two parties. Once she is able to transform the conflict into a problem, she looks for ways to resolve it by peaceful means. She says that this is what the public expects of her. From this vantage point, she probably sees a conflict in school in the same way. The reason she feels this way (despite the fact that a school leader is not a judge) is probably anchored in her belief that there are sufficient laws, rules, and regulations to guide the school leader in managing and adjudicating conflicts that arise in school.

School leaders should serve as a model of behavior while working on a conflict. Perhaps the judge feels that if she behaves "properly" in court (succinctly, truthfully, and politely when questioning a witness) the lawyers will act the same. We know that she wants it to be that way because at times emotions flare up. Perhaps that is why she feels that this is an effective method of behaving in schools, as well.

THE CHORAL CONDUCTOR'S TWO RECOMMENDATIONS FOR MAKING BENEFICIAL USE OF STUDENTS' ACHIEVEMENT DATA

School leaders should praise the students for their achievement test scores and explain the meanings of the scores in order to expand the sense of ownership of the scores. This recommendation derives directly from the conductor's own work. He feels that praising the work of the chorus and explaining what the chorus sings and the quality of singing it achieves are of utmost importance. With this recommendation, the conductor perhaps views the school as equivalent to his chorus and the student test scores as equivalent to his concerts.

School leaders should do their best to analyze student achievement scores and use them to guide teachers on how to improve student learning. This recommendation also stems from the conductor's work. He uses such analysis to motivate singers and improve the quality of future performances. He feels that school leaders ought to do the same with teachers.

13

A Method to Examine the Validity of the Recommendations

A survey was sent to practicing school leaders asking for their opinions about these twenty-four recommendations. The format used in the questioning was as follows:

> A [title of the professional making the recommendation] recommends that school leaders should [one or more verbs] [one or more related items].
> Is this recommendation useful? Yes? No? Maybe?
> Why?
> Is it feasible to implement this recommendation? Yes? No? Maybe?
> Why?

This is not the first time that "out-of the-box lenses" are used for the purpose of learning more about competencies that school leaders need to possess and use in their job. For example, in the recent past, attempts have been made to conceptually apply broadly articulated "out-of-the-box" theories and principles to school leadership (i.e., Connerley and Pedersen 2005).

These attempts, however, have not included checking out the practical relevance of the theories with practitioners. We wanted to test that and hopefully apply specific "out-of-the-box" recommendations to the complex practice of school leadership (Green 2005; Starratt 2003). What we will now do is examine the usefulness and feasibility (relevance and applicability) of the specific recommendations offered by the external specialists to a number of school leaders, realizing full well that the relevance and applicability would depend heavily on how the recommendations might become integrated into specific contexts.

To carry this study, permission was sought to survey a number of school leaders about their feelings regarding each of the twenty-four recommendations made by the eight professionals. Permission was obtained from the School Board of California's largest 9–12 high school district (enrolled over 33,000 students in the 2004–2005 school year) and from the School Board of California's largest K–8 elementary and middle school district (enrolled over 29,000 students in the 2004–2005 school year).

Once permission was received, each of the two district's central offices received one envelope with the questionnaires. In each case the assistant superintendent for instruction sent one questionnaire to each of the forty-seven high school principals and assistant principals in the 9–12 district and to each of the forty-two principals in the K–8 district. All (100 percent) of the forty-seven school leaders in the former group and thirty-five (close to 82 percent) of the forty-two leaders in the latter group completed and returned the questionnaires anonymously to their respective district offices.

Each questionnaire was sent with a cover letter that briefly described the researcher. The letter outlined the purpose of the survey and emphasized the potential value of the information gathered over and above what researchers already know about the topic. Possible benefits to the respondents and their colleagues from the gathered information were also mentioned. Confidentiality was pledged. A promise was made to share the data with them once they were compiled and analyzed. The total turnaround time lasted close to two months, from early September to late October of 2004.

Among the secondary school leaders, ideally there would have been a total of 2,056 responses (47 respondents times 24 recommendations times 2 criteria—usefulness and feasibility). But in 102 instances (4.52 percent of a total possible 2,056 responses), respondents did not answer one or more of the items. Of those 102 cases, 91 were related to the position the respondent took regarding "feasibility," and 11 were related to "usefulness" (90 percent and 10 percent, respectively). The blanks were taken to imply "maybe" responses and were so recorded.

As for the elementary school leaders, 1,680 responses would have been possible (35 responses times 24 recommendations times 2 criteria of applicability to school leadership). But in 130 cases (7.15 percent of the total possible 1,680 responses), respondents did not answer one or more of the items. Of those 130 instances, 96 were related to the position the respondent took regarding "feasibility," and 33 were related to "usefulness" (74 percent and 26 percent, respectively). As with the secondary school leaders, here, too, the blanks were taken to imply "maybe" responses, and they were so recorded.

The next chapter depicts the total number of responses recorded as "yes," "no," and "maybe" for each recommendation, noted separately for secondary and elementary school leaders (no differentiation made between principals and assistant principals). Additionally, examples of reasons provided by respondents are given for the positions they took. The reasons reported represent the range of reasons given for each response. This range was determined by content analysis and detection of themes found in all of the reasons given. The order in which the data are presented parallels the earlier order used in describing the interviews with the specialists and their recommendations.

14

School Leaders React to the Recommendations

This chapter summarizes the reactions that school leaders had to the specialists' recommendations. The summary for each recommendation includes (separately for "usefulness" and for "feasibility" and separately for secondary school leaders and for elementary school leaders) the following: total number of "yes" answers, "no" answers, and "maybe" answers and examples of reasons given for the answer.

PREDETERMINED SCHOOL GOALS: THE AIRLINE CAPTAIN

Recommendation 1: Assistant Principalship Should Be Required

Usefulness

Secondary school leaders (SSL): 47 yes. Experience is the best training. This allows for being exposed to various roles in the school with relatively little risk. One can learn school and district operations. Newly appointed principals can quickly learn the job, the procedures, and the culture.

Elementary school leaders (ESL): 32 yes, 1 no, 2 maybe. This provides for valuable practical experience, understanding of the big picture, a learning base, and familiarity with all the steps. One learns policies and procedures with a mentor.

Feasibility

SSL: 44 yes, 1 no, 2 maybe. This is a required job pattern. This is a board and district policy. The pool of candidates is too small. It depends on the school size.

123

ESL: 26 yes, 9 maybe. It should be a policy. This depends on the size of the district and the schools. It is a function of the number of available positions.

Recommendation 2: Staff Meetings for New Employees

Usefulness

SSL: 27 yes, 16 no, 4 maybe. New hires should become familiar with the organization, its policies, and its issues. It would be part of team building. This can be done more effectively in other ways, like e-mail. This is relevant only if it is a high-level appointment.

ESL: 5 yes, 23 no, 7 maybe. This is a communication vehicle that builds cohesiveness. It helps establish norms. It is needed because of staff changes. This is a waste of time away from instruction. Others do not need the information. This is overkill. One could use other ways to inform.

Feasibility

SSL: 18 yes, 22 no, 7 maybe. It takes too much of everyone's time. Typically, there is ongoing hiring throughout the school year, and convening such meetings would be impossible. This is possible only in a small school.

ESL: 8 yes, 20 no, 7 maybe. This is an administrator's decision. There are time constraints. Teachers can help before the administrator does.

Recommendation 3: Take Responsibility for Problems before Communicating Them

Usefulness

SSL: 25 yes, 15 no, 7 maybe. This is a job requirement. Owning the problem improves communication. It promotes a smooth operation and team collaboration. This facilitates problem solving, including when delegation occurs.

ESL: 16 yes, 6 no, 13 maybe. This is part of what you are supposed to do. The principal is accountable. Leaders need to know both the problem and the solution before letting the people know that they care. One need not blame oneself unnecessarily.

Feasibility

SSL: 23 yes, 18 no, 6 maybe. Leaders are required to do it. This encourages dialogue. This provides assurances that save time in the long run. One must look at the big picture instead. There is a need to delegate and not waste time. This speeds up gossip.

ESL: 16 yes, 4 no, 15 maybe. This is an issue. It depends.

Recommendation 4: Establish These Priorities: Safety, Comfort, Schedule, and Efficiency

Usefulness

SSL: 34 yes, 5 no, 8 maybe. Safety is the most important consideration. Priorities 2 to 4 are critical but vary according to specific situations.

ESL: 27 yes, 1 no, 7 maybe. Safety comes first. Safety is top priority, even before learning. Comfort can be negotiated. It depends on the problem and its urgency. Learning time is very valuable.

Feasibility

SSL: 22 yes, 14 no, 11 maybe. Safety is so important that it is mentioned in the job description, and it is also on the school leader's mind all the time. School people need as much support as possible for the maintenance of safety. There is no such policy. There cannot be one unless it is measured within the context of the working environment.

ESL: 20 yes, 2 no, 13 maybe. Sacrifice everything for safety. Children's comfort is so important for learning that you have to work with teachers on that. How do you define efficiency?

Recommendation 5: Screened Principalship Candidates for Autonomy

Usefulness

SSL: 29 yes, 12 no, 6 maybe. It is a leadership trait that needs to be looked at legally. This needs to be seriously examined. There is no good measure of school leadership. The principal's work is teamwork.

ESL: 15 yes, 5 no, 15 maybe. A leader has to make decisions under such circumstances. This should be part of the job description. Hiring decisions should be made on the basis of this as well as on the basis of collaborative work.

Feasibility

SSL: 29 yes, 11 no, 7 maybe. With some better work on assessing autonomy, it should be feasible.

ESL: 17 yes, 7 no, 11 maybe. This is already done. The district includes it. It is done but is probably different for different schools. There may not be time.

SAFETY AND RULE ENFORCEMENT: THE TRAFFIC POLICE OFFICER

Recommendation 6: Be Visible

Usefulness

SSL: 43 yes, 1 no, 3 maybe. Part of the job requirement. Prevents fighting and other unacceptable behaviors. Provides a calming effect. Improves moral behavior.

ESL: 35 yes. This is managing by walking around (MBWA). It is proactive, eliminates problems before they happen, diffuses and reduces conflicts, and helps in solving long-range problems. This keeps everyone on task. It increases compliance. It helps to gain understanding. This is important for staff and parents, too. It is useful but needs quality time. This is extremely necessary, but it causes stress.

Feasibility

SSL: 26 yes, 9 no, 12 maybe. You must. Simply make it at least 20 percent of your time. It is easy to do. Cannot always take time. At least one member of the team should do it.

ESL: 24 yes, 4 no, 7 maybe. Just prioritize use of time for the day. Engage in that just before and just after school. Show leadership by being there. Do as much as you can, but do not sacrifice other important things. Do it with concern, interest, control, and commitment. Delegate.

Recommendation 7: Become Comfortable with Acting from a Position of Authority

Usefulness

SSL: 43 yes, 1 no, 3 maybe. Why be in a leadership position if you cannot do it? Others look to you in that capacity. Being comfortable helps the leader make decisions and be a team leader; it helps to make people feel at ease. Authority provides power to act. One must not abuse power. It enables one to make tough decisions for the good of the whole school. This allows for strong site and participatory management.

ESL: 30 yes, 5 maybe. The buck stops with the leader. It is essential for good decision making. It provides personal security and respect. This enhances your image, and it is necessary for personal power and influence. Parents need to know it. Yes, but one also needs to be comfortable with being a person that possesses authority—not just with acting from a position of authority. Not always. Perhaps this is needed for the No Child Left Behind legislation.

Feasibility

SSL: 30 yes, 6 no, 11 maybe. It is good hiring practice. It should be part of training. No question about it. You have to learn what decisiveness means. You must be willing to be comfortable; it does not happen by itself. Develop self-confidence. Remember that emotions sometimes may be on the sleeve. It depends on staff support.

ESL: 29 yes, 6 maybe. We are already in a position of authority, and we could not be so without being comfortable. You need to intensify your interactions with the staff.

Recommendation 8: Need to Collaborate and Eliminate Confusion

Usefulness

SSL: 41 yes, 3 no, 3 maybe. Codependency is a fact. Cooperation promotes understanding. It streamlines services. It provides smooth transitions. Collaboration contributes to safety. This maximizes potential but also confusion. Integrated services help students.

ESL: 30 yes, 5 maybe. Our schools need the related agencies. This is advantageous to students and staff. It takes a village to raise a child. This is a noble goal. You need to work together to fulfill the needs that children have. A family atmosphere gives better results. It speeds processes. If confusion is decreased, then productivity increases.

Feasibility

SSL: 16 yes, 17 no, 14 maybe. Work on communication. Learn to rely on each other. Need district support for it. Clarity eliminates confusion. There are policies and procedures for collaborations. You have to change the landscape of the district and state goals. It should become part of the school-site safety reports. This is too complex and takes too much work. There are time constraints. Some agencies come to you with incomplete agendas and different degrees of open-door policies.

ESL: 24 yes, 11 maybe. This is the case by virtue of being authorized by various levels of government. It develops with experience. These are complex processes, and they do not always materialize. The feasibility would depend on how clear the authorities are.

Recommendation 9: Leaders Must Show Teachers How to Act from a Position of Authority

Usefulness

SSL: 41 yes, 2 no, 4 maybe. Teachers need to lead classrooms. Students seek direction. Classroom discipline is imperative for effective learning to take place. It would be useful only if authority is under clearly established policies. Teachers must feel supported. Principals must empower teachers. When teachers feel comfortable with authority then the school is strong. This allows the community to communicate well with the school.

ESL: 28 yes, 3 no, 4 maybe. It improves discipline and, thus, there is more time on task. Parents need assurance and confidence. It helps teachers gain respect. Students need to know who is in charge. Teachers need it, but they also have to work hard and display enthusiasm. It could eliminate sending students to the office.

Feasibility

SSL: 31 yes, 4 no, 12 maybe. Principals could help within the context of staff development. Provide training on authority and responsibility by working on competence and confidence. It requires a certain type of personality. It is difficult to do because at times teachers who are comfortable working with authority abuse their authority. It is difficult to achieve from the outside of a person. This is too complex because there are too many agendas and egos.

ESL: 21 yes, 3 no, 11 maybe. You help by supporting them. The principal needs to share leadership. It can help them if you yourself exercise your authority with compassion.

Recommendation 10: Need to Become Fully Aware of What Is Occurring, the Related Law, and the Consequences (When Law Enforcement Is on Campus)

Usefulness

SSL: 45 yes, 1 no, 1 maybe. You need to know what transpired, the charges, and who is responsible. You must deal with security issues; a school safety plan helps facilitate safety and resolve conflicts. The leader has to have reliable information. You need to protect the rights of everyone. The principal has to respond to questions. You have to instill confidence.

ESL: 25 yes, 2 no, 8 maybe. This is mandatory. It is important for school safety. There is no need to know it all. This is too much to know. This relates to our clientele.

Feasibility

SSL: 26 yes, 11 no, 10 maybe. You learn the law and the reasons why the cops are on campus. You work with the officers. Call for help. Communicate well with the law-enforcement personnel. School law classes are available. Dean of students deals with these issues if the law is not violated.

School law and public law do not always reconcile. The campus is too big with too many situations. You cannot know it all. The laws are changing.

ESL: 19 yes, 4 no, 12 maybe. Expect help. All visitors have to know that when they come to campus, they have to check with the office. The cops should phone before they come. This knowledge comes with experience. You learn material that relates to safety. It is impossible to know it all. There are tons of laws and codes. What about efficiency? What about conflicting obligations?

Recommendation 11: Need to Promptly Interpret and Apply District Rules

Usefulness

SSL: 45 yes, 1 no, 1 maybe. You need it for effective site management, especially for keeping safety and order. It promotes consistency. Principals need to do that in order to communicate them to the public.

ESL: 28 yes, 7 maybe. You really need these things. It brings about consistency and fairness.

Feasibility

SSL: 33 yes, 5 no, 9 maybe. Knowledge is a prerequisite. Learn where to seek answers. You need to develop a clear code of personal ethics. You have to think through the procedures. Enforce by modeling. Actually there are very few gray areas. District does a good job in terms of clarity. The guidelines are clear. Knowledge is gained from experience. The school is too big. This is not easy. You cannot really be effective without staff development.

ESL: 21 yes, 2 no, 12 maybe. This is a basic responsibility that we all carry out. You learn by reviewing control and regulations. One simple way to do it is to set standards. It is not so simple because you cannot violate student rights. But there is a need to be open, too. Political factors play into this.

ENHANCING STUDENT BENEFITS: THE CROP GROWER

Recommendation 12: Reducing Interference with Learning

Usefulness

SSL: 27 yes, 8 no, 12 maybe. This is a central component of managing a school. The public and the parents expect that. Minimum interferences increase outcomes. Acting authoritatively and with a constant eye for efficiency is inappropriate for schools.

ESL: 17 yes, 7 no, 11 maybe. Less disruption leads to more learning. This keeps the overall priorities in the forefront. Good to be aware of. It helps to maintain an academic campus. Growth will always be an issue.

Feasibility

SSL: 15 yes, 29 no, 3 maybe. One needs to learn how to plan. You cannot do it with your limited authority and control. Not everything is the principal's responsibility. There is not enough funding. Overcrowded classrooms make it impossible.

ESL: 12 yes, 10 no, 13 maybe. You look for areas in which attempts to minimize interferences bring about the strongest effects on learning. It is difficult to accomplish in a school that has over five hundred students. This is possible only to some degree.

Recommendation 13: Emphasize Preparation for Job and Higher Education in School's Curriculum

Usefulness

SSL: 32 yes, 7 no, 8 maybe. That is what education is founded on. We need vocational education. The curriculum must reflect needs of kids and communities. It would alleviate overcrowding. I disagree with the premise that the purpose of education is to prepare for the labor market.

ESL: 11 yes, 8 no, 16 maybe. This is good for students. Work and career are closely related to education. The end products are important—higher education and jobs. The labor market does not make considerations for the individual's education; rather, the individual needs to be prepared to compete in a free market. Perhaps high schools and middle schools can do it, not us. These are not the only criteria for educating citizens. Our standards dictate the curriculum.

Feasibility

SSL: 12 yes, 14 no, 21 maybe. You need to work with local labor leaders through local boards. Continually test all programs for productivity. Develop a three- to five-year vision, and plan for that rather than react. To learn the ever-changing markets and quality of life and to tie to the school programs is very difficult—actually, no way! It all depends on funding.

ESL: 8 yes, 12 no, 15 maybe. There are so many specific things that you can do along these lines. The relationship between the experiences in elementary schools and higher education and jobs is very difficult to determine. State standards are limiting what you can do, but you can negotiate delaying them.

HELPING TO SOLVE PROBLEMS: THE SERVICE ADVISOR

Recommendation 14: Need to Reflect on Decisions and How to Communicate Them

Usefulness

SSL: 46 yes, 1 no. We do that all the time with students, staff, parents, and the public. Communication is situational. It depends on the audience level, range, and numbers. Communication is a tool for having people agree with your decision. Verbal communication with emotion is needed sometimes in emergency situations.

ESL: 27 yes, 2 no, 6 maybe. This helps demonstrate clearly what leadership is. It has to be part of the qualifications for the job. This relates to clientele. It demonstrates awareness. Communication is the key. These skills assist with anticipating how the customer will react to the decision. It helps when problems arise with the decision. People are different.

Feasibility

SSL: 31 yes, 2 no, 14 maybe. Develop self-awareness about style, confidence, and success of communication. Develop pool of evaluating principals. It has to be a function of time, but not everyone is successful. Need training, perhaps.

ESL: 21 yes, 5 no, 9 maybe. Share factual information, but do it at different levels. Be consistent with the evidence and flexible as you show it, depending on what the customer wants to know. Communicate quickly and with a cool head. Be wise. When I changed from a small high school to a big high school, I began communicating mainly by e-mail, and I don't see why I have to worry because a decision is a decision. You need to learn how to do it, but not everyone can do it.

Recommendation 15: Learn How to Market the School

Usefulness

SSL: 39 yes, 3 no, 5 maybe. It helps to attract students. To be a salesman is number one. You need to market your products. Image is important to parents and community, especially when a school bond has to be passed. This is an important tool for funding, especially in lower-income schools. Schools need to continue to operate regardless of the whimsical public perceptions. PR is one of the most important tasks. The public needs to know about curricula, instruction, and programs. Accountability calls for it.

ESL: 26 yes, 1 no, 8 maybe. We have the students, and we do not need to market. We need to advertise so that we get public support. Principals must sell within and outside. Success breeds success. Without it effective schools will suffer. Public image is important. No sales. I am not sure about the need for that.

Feasibility

SSL: 21 yes, 5 no, 21 maybe. Simply describe what you do daily; that is selling. Website. Increase the school's visibility. Talk the talk and walk the walk. Establish a public-information unit. Advertise student performance. Learn to be prepared to answer questions with confidence. Hire a public-relations firm. No matter what you say, some schools have a bad image because of where they are located. You cannot control media.

ESL: 23 yes, 2 no, 10 maybe. Develop enthusiasm for the school and for student achievement. Work out ways to celebrate successes and accomplishments. Encourage participation and attendance. Work with the PTA. There is no time for it. We already do what we have to do. Experience may help.

Recommendation 16: Learn to Make Decisions More from the Heart

Usefulness

SSL: 11 yes, 24 no, 12 maybe. Administrators fear such decisions but must take into account anomalies. The job is 80 percent human resources. Yes, we are here to serve kids. You need to always give the benefit of the doubt. No, there is already a balance between heart and rules, and it has to be preserved. Emotional decisions tend to be inaccurate. In large districts it is the policy that is important. No, because one must make decisions for the school as a whole, and it may conflict with decisions from the heart about individual students. Must run school as a business with its philosophy and culture. Legal consequences may not allow it. Law and procedures established by the board cannot be compromised. Inconsistency creates problems.

ESL: 19 yes, 4 no, 12 maybe. Most of us are already doing it. People don't care what you know until they know that you care. Justice is a messy dilemma. There must be a proper mix. Decide with a strong—not a bleeding—heart. You need to take everything into consideration but abide by the rules. Need should prevail over heart. You need to follow the law. You need to avoid impulsiveness. It may be a bad precedent. It may lead to wrong decisions. You may not take things personally.

Feasibility

SSL: 8 yes, 19 no, 20 maybe. Hire administrators with a value system in mind. Use rationality, vision, data, and experience. You must abide by state laws and mandates. See to it that you never compromise the institution.

Heart cannot be taught. Cannot use the heart too much because it is not always fair.

ESL: 18 yes, 7 no, 10 maybe. We should capitalize more on the many informal opportunities to do it. Work on integrating it with what you have to do. Use the heart as much as needed, but do not let it dictate the decision. Balancing is difficult. It is possible only in certain times.

ASSUMING FIDUCIARY RESPONSIBILITY: THE CFO

Recommendation 17: Budgetary Knowledge

Usefulness

SSL: 38 yes, 6 no, 3 maybe. You need to make maximum use of limited funds for kids and for the public to know. You have to be able to answer questions. Most decisions principals make depend on the budget. Finances are behind most decisions. Maximum knowledge is needed. You must know budgetary issues at all levels of government. Knowing your financial workings informs your allocation decisions. We do not necessarily need more. Instead we need more knowledge about facility management. This is a lower priority than student achievement.

ESL: 27 yes, 3 no, 5 maybe. This helps to know what resources you have, how to maximize them, and how to best use them in school. It is good for efficiency and for educating all students. It is vital to articulate the budget into effective programs. This will increase achievement. To keep fiscal solvency is a high priority. This must be a part of promotion of the school. Well, most school budgets are prepared for the entire year. This is not applicable for ordinary budgets. There is no time for all of this. It is enough for principals to just be instructional leaders.

Feasibility

SSL: 20 yes, 15 no, 12 maybe. The district should pay for professional development. You can gain needed knowledge in a variety of ways. Seeking out too many resources and meeting the requirements about how to spend becomes inefficient. Not everyone has to be knowledgeable in all areas, including finances. Each one of us has our expertise. All of that might make sense only if the district gives school principals more significant budgetary authorities.

ESL: 22 yes, 3 no, 10 maybe. We need staff development. Training should be provided. There is no need to become a CFO. Whatever is needed comes with experience.

PROVIDING COMFORT: THE HOSPITAL CHAPLAIN

Recommendation 18: Develop Intuitiveness, Spontaneity, and Communicative Skills

Usefulness

SSL: 42 yes, 1 no, 4 maybe. Spontaneity is critical because of the day-to-day surprises. You have to say and do what is needed. It is underappreciated, but because of multiple needs, that is precisely what we have to do and we do. We are in the people business. The more skills, the better the communication.

ESL: 28 yes, 7 maybe. Yes, because you deal with people daily. This is a good blend. The key. Communication must be clear. Not sure if spontaneity and intuition are necessary.

Feasibility

SSL: 22 yes, 9 no, 16 maybe. If you don't have them, you then work on them. Staff development. There is no room for emotions; we need to be professional. No, because these are qualities that are sometimes difficult to define. How can I learn to be calm when I want to help? Emotions have no room here, just professional behavior. You've got to watch what you say. Not sure.

ESL: 26 yes, 1 no, 8 maybe. These are qualifications that must come with the job. Learn to go with the flow and enjoy what you do. Intelligence and eloquence are fine, but without wisdom you are dead meat. It comes with experience.

Recommendation 19: School Leaders Should Be Hired If They Love People, Learning, and Teaching

Usefulness

SSL: 47 yes. This underlies everything you are doing. It is assumed in the job.

ESL: 29 yes, 6 maybe. This is education, pure and simple. This is a must, and if it is lacking, then you need to think about it more in relation to the job.

Feasibility

SSL: 31 yes, 3 no, 13 maybe. I have been doing it for a long time, and I can tell you that anyone can learn to love. Work to strengthen it. It takes a lot of self-reflection. If you are asking about teachers, these are qualities to check out when hiring, but once the person is tenured, forget about it. It is just impossible to think about providing comfort to everyone who needs it in the school.

ESL: 27 yes, 8 maybe. Sure, it is feasible, most of us love it all. Work on it every day to do it right. Priests may love everybody, and frankly, I don't know how to do it. If it is not a proper screening for evaluation, what is? I am not sure. You should respect it all but "love"?

MANAGING AND ADJUDICATING CONFLICTS: THE COURTROOM JUDGE

Recommendation 20: Learn about a Conflict before Getting Involved

Usefulness

SSL: 43 yes, 3 no, 1 maybe. Information is critical to making a good judgment. Knowledge is power. Absolutely. Proper research of mediation techniques is important. No; you need to get involved for safety issues. Get involved as you learn.

ESL: 24 yes, 4 no, 7 maybe. This is obviously useful; it is automatic with the job. The background of the problem helps. You need the details. Knowledge is powerful. You need to make informed choices. This will help to save face. No, because how do you know if the knowledge you had before you heard the parties represents everybody? You often have to act immediately in a clearly defined way and so get more knowledge once you start hearing everybody.

Feasibility

SSL: 25 yes, 8 no, 14 maybe. Gather facts from as many sources as possible. We confront conflicts daily, and we do that daily. Encourage communication. Take the needed time. Comes with experience, like serving as dean first.

ESL: 19 yes, 6 no, 10 maybe. Yes, learn the issues well first. You have to think it through. Review the procedures. If not before, then learn later. Weigh the costs. Avoid legal problems. You don't always have the time. Not sure.

Recommendation 21: Turn Conflicts into Problems to Be Solved by Amicable Means

Usefulness

SSL: 41 yes, 2 no, 4 maybe. This creates win-win situations. That is the goal of conflict resolution. This is the art of administration. Necessary. Confrontation occurs daily, and this is our business: people. Reduces fighting incidences.

ESL: 27 yes, 8 maybe. Yes, because people you confront do not go away. You need to continue the relationship after the conflict. This is a must. It is needed to build support. It provides structure. Attitude goes a long way. Amicable is not the only way.

Feasibility

SSL: 19 yes, 8 no, 20 maybe. Use diplomacy. Teach students to solve their problems. All issues may not be solved, but you must try over and over again. We need staff development. Use peer mediation. I cannot solve it all because there is no time. Even if you are not successful, then try to explain, especially to parents. Sometimes an illegal action must be dealt with "not amicably."

ESL: 25 yes, 1 no, 9 maybe. You need to counsel students first. Learn conflict resolution. It does not always work.

Recommendation 22: Model Proper Behavior while Working on a Conflict

Usefulness

SSL: 46 yes, 1 maybe. It provides one with credibility. This is a powerful example. Most people who are in a conflict situation probably have not had positive role models. The principal must not lose composure. This is always good for administrative leadership. The process sometimes is more important than the results.

ESL: 29 yes, 6 maybe. Must model expected behaviors. Being a model is an integral part of teaching. Everything that adults do is a model for children. Others learn from you.

Feasibility

SSL: 33 yes, 1 no, 13 maybe. Need to develop it. Need training. It involves thinking extra hard before acting. You have to develop a commitment to something like that. Important features include exercising self-control and staying calm. Develop your listening skills. Being compassionate helps to become a model. Not everyone is perfect on that. Difficult.

ESL: 27 yes, 2 no, 6 maybe. Walk the talk. Get training. Model especially during an intervention; it's the best time to do it. Develop the attitude for it, and learn to persevere.

MAKING BENEFICIAL USES OF ACHIEVEMENT DATA: THE CHORAL CONDUCTOR

Recommendation 23: Need to Praise Achievement and Interpret the Meanings of Test Scores with Charisma

Usefulness

SSL: 42 yes, 1 no, 4 maybe. You have to explain what scores really mean. Media can be misleading. It gains trust, respect, credibility, and faith in the leadership. This will encourage parents and public involvement. We are in the public eye. It is the role of all of us, not just the administrators, teachers and others, too.

ESL: 23 yes, 1 no, 11 maybe. You are the leader, aren't you? The public at large needs to understand our procedures and issues. You need to be able to educate the community. You have to develop pride in the workplace. The public wants to know that kids are safe and learning. The public judges us mercilessly. That would help, despite numbers. It helps during times of change.

Feasibility

SSL: 26 yes, 10 no, 11 maybe. It costs nothing. The activities can be easily accomplished, but not everyone is highly charismatic.

ESL: 23 yes, 3 no, 9 maybe. Use data and public relations. You must provide accurate information. If you believe in what you are promoting, you can do it. Hit the correct people. We need to stand up and ask for help. Not sure. It depends a lot on the scores.

Recommendation 24: Use Student Scores to Guide Teachers' Work

Usefulness

SSL: 44 yes, 1 no, 4 maybe. In this age of accountability, data analysis is extremely important, both for the educators and the lay people. It gains public support for what the staff is doing. Schools are judged by these data. So much emphasis is placed on assessment and test scores. This is one of the most important qualities of a school leader. All leaders must have these skills, but few have them.

ESL: 30 yes, 5 maybe. Growth is important. People need to know what the challenges are. Accountability. This is part of the job. Absolutely. School reform depends on it. It helps teachers. This is the right way.

Feasibility

SSL: 29 yes, 5 no, 13 maybe. Need training. This should be a criterion for hiring a principal. Data-test-retest-evaluate-change program. Learn to use tools to understand how data drives the decisions in schools. Practice. You must dish out the information that is really relevant. This is part of what we do. Make time because there are only twenty-four hours a day.

ESL: 29 yes, 2 no, 4 maybe. If decline occurs, then auditing can focus on how to continue growth. All the departments and the schools should work together. It is a district effort. Communicate with the district on that. Work smarter. We do it informally. Answer the teachers' questions. Training if it becomes a nationwide commitment.

IV

LESSONS: HOW TO IMPROVE
SCHOOL-LEADERSHIP
ACCOUNTABILITY

15

What the Data Imply

Overall, the findings reported in the last chapter regarding the acceptability by school leaders of the recommendations offered to them by the specialists show the following:

1. Most school leaders perceived most of the recommendations as useful.
2. A significant but somewhat smaller number of school leaders saw the implementation of several of the recommendations as being feasible.
3. The reasons given by school leaders for "yes" answers on usefulness were more plentiful and appeared more convincing in most cases than the reasons given for "no" answers.
4. Regardless of the answer given about the feasibility of any given recommendation, school leaders offered numerous suggestions for making the implementation of many recommendations feasible.

The recommendations that we chose to include in the survey seemed to us to be both useful and feasible. Furthermore, we note again that our sample of respondents was not representative of the overall population of school leaders. Thus, all we can offer here are some general findings of our survey, some tentative explanations for these findings, and some suggestions to school leaders regarding general principles of improving school leader accountability. These principles are offered as reactions to "no" or "maybe" answers that school leaders gave regarding the usefulness and the feasibility of some of the recommendations offered by the specialists.

CHALLENGE 1—ACHIEVING PREDETERMINED GOALS

The airline captain specializes in flying passengers toward a predetermined destination. He made five recommendations that relate to the achievement of predetermined school goals. A large majority of the school leaders agreed with the usefulness and feasibility of the first recommendation, namely, that one needs to serve as an assistant principal before serving as a principal. School district leaders should be made aware of this finding. The captain spoke of the experience that a second in command gains while serving alongside a first in command. He also spoke about the second in command undertaking some leadership duties in less complex situations (over ten thousand feet in the air, where the air traffic is relatively low).

If the captain's recommendation about the second in command is not followed in schools then the following might happen. Upon becoming principals, those principals without an assistant principalship experience would have a major disadvantage. They would be assuming all of the responsibilities of a principal and be expected to be accountable for them without first having assumed responsibilities for at least some of them and being accountable for them, as is the situation for an assistant principal. To be placed in such a situation without the prior experience of being an assistant principal is difficult, stressful, and probably unjustified.

The recommendation about having staff members meet as a group with every new member seemed not to be applicable in the eyes of several school leaders. Less than half of the secondary school group and only one in seven of the elementary school group saw it as useful. As to feasibility, only about one-third of the combined groups saw it as such. A common reason given for a "no" answer regarding the usefulness of this recommendation was that staff members prefer to orient and get to know their new colleagues in other ways.

But there is plenty to learn from this captain's mindset on this issue. Any new staff member, at least at the beginning, must buy into the predetermined school goals or the achievement of them could be compromised. Predetermined school goals are usually long-range ones, and there are no other schoolwide forums in which they are discussed. For the captain, the landing destination is the long-range goal, and everyone on the aircraft needs to work toward this end. For school leaders, achieving predetermined school goals is a long-range process, and everyone in the school needs to be on the same page in this regard.

Assuming responsibility for a problem before communicating it to others was the captain's third recommendation. About half of the surveyed school practitioners saw the recommendation as useful. Fewer people considered it feasible. Most "no" answers on usefulness and on feasibility focused on either taking responsibility for problems ("Not every problem is the school leader's problem") or on communicating the problem ("Why communicate about the problem if it is not yet solved?"). None of the "no" answers were accompanied by reasons related to both the "problem own-ership" dimension and the "problem communication" dimension.

Again, we wish to point to the captain's mindset, as we understand it. A problematic situation that is not yet solved might bring about a sense of un-certainty to those who hear about it. Communicating to others that re-sponsibility for the issue has been assumed might reduce the anxiety stem-ming from uncertainty. The road to achieving schoolwide goals may be filled with problems. School leaders' accountability could be enhanced if school staff members knew that the leader has assumed responsibility for those problems, particularly ones that affect the staff directly.

From the reasons that school leaders gave for their "yes," "no," or "maybe" answers regarding usefulness of the fourth recommendation (i.e., prioritiz-ing concerns when a serious problem occurs), the following might be gath-ered. All respondents agreed with the captain that "safety" is number 1. A large majority agreed that "comfort" is number 2. He ranked "schedule" as number 3 and "efficiency" as number 4. Some school leaders felt that "com-fort" is less important than "not interrupting the learning schedule." Perhaps these respondents need to rethink the possible effect of student comfort (and discomfort) on learning.

As for efficiency, many respondents considered it as not belonging to the most-important-factors list altogether. One school leader asked, "How do you define it?" Another said, "There is no such policy." Such questions may suggest that those leaders become more aware of the need to achieve goals given the available resources in order to become more accountable.

About half of the respondents said "yes" to the usefulness of the recom-mendation that, during job interviews, candidates should be screened for autonomy. School district officials should become aware of such thinking even though decentralizing authority to school leaders has governance and bureaucratic implications.

CHALLENGE 2—ASSURING SAFETY AND ADHERENCE TO RULES

The traffic police officer offered six recommendations that focused on how to improve safety and rule enforcement. These recommendations included being visible, being comfortable acting from a position of authority, coor-dinating with others in order to minimize confusion, helping teachers to become comfortable acting from authority, being aware of everything when law-enforcement personnel are on campus, and knowing how to interpret district policies.

All six recommendations were seen as useful by an overwhelming ma-jority of the school leaders. Somewhat smaller percentages of "yes" an-swers were given with regard to feasibility. Those who did not see some of the recommendations as being feasible mentioned the following reasons: lack of sufficient time, excessive responsibility without concomitant authority, ambiguities in the policies, lack of sufficient knowledge about the law, and lack of comfort in dealing with the feelings of others.

Perhaps some school leaders need to improve their time-management skills. With specific regard to being visible, it might be useful to patrol potential trouble spots in order to "smell" trouble and potential trouble and perhaps even get others to help patrol in order to increase administrative visibility.

Possible abuse of power seems to concern many school leaders in relationship to acting from a position of authority. Similar concerns were expressed with regard to empowering teachers to act from a position of authority. Such reluctance might reduce the staff's effectiveness in these areas. Leaders might wish to learn how to develop and maintain a balance between the need to be clear, concise, and decisive and the need to show sensitivity, empathy, and understanding.

This dilemma is common in education, particularly when the authority figure is unarmed and without a police badge. This police officer appeared to be no less sensitive than many educators are. But he also radiated a strong sense of authority and decisiveness regarding the tasks that he had to accomplish. He said that this attitude and behavior improved with experience. The officer appeared to have knowledge, a rational mindset, a clear orientation toward his work, and an ability to "read" and care about people.

The officer recommended that school leaders increase their knowledge of the law and become better aware of how the law should be interpreted. Half of the surveyed practitioners wrote that they agree with this assertion. Some disagreed with it because they felt that the campus is too big, and there are too many legal situations to consider and handle. One said, "There are tons of laws and codes; you cannot know them all." Another respondent said, "Laws are changing." A third person said, "I have conflicting obligations." They did not elaborate.

Perhaps short-term "residencies" spent with appropriate district officials, experienced school leaders, law-enforcement personnel, or legal experts are in order for those school leaders who need this assistance. Such residencies should include useful updates and workshops that would improve the leader's capacity to be accountable in the area of safety and rule enforcement.

CHALLENGE 3—PRODUCING WELL-PREPARED STUDENTS

One might despair when looking at the limited school leaders' "yes" responses to the two recommendations made by the crop grower, particularly the responses regarding feasibility:

1. For looking at problems in school as interference with learning, "usefulness" showed 27 out of 47 of the secondary school group and 17 out of 35 of the elementary school group responding "yes." "Feasibility" showed 15 out of 47 of the secondary school group and 12 out of 35 of the elementary school group responding "yes."
2. For designing curriculum suitable for preparing students for jobs and higher education, "usefulness" showed 32 out of 47 of the secondary school group and 11 out of 33 of the elementary school group responding "yes." Feasibility showed 12 out of 47 of the secondary school group and 8 out of 35 of the elementary school group responding "yes."

The crop grower calls for fine-tuning solutions to learning problems and for establishing a curriculum that meets the demand of the market and of higher education. Many of those surveyed did not like that way of viewing education, nor did they see it as useful.

Perhaps these reactions could have been predicted from these school leaders who work predominantly with children from low socioeconomic backgrounds, and many of who have learning difficulties (i.e., by high school). Some secondary school leaders wrote that it is too late to fix learning problems. Two elementary school leaders wrote that academic fundamentals are needed, not specializations for future work or study.

The issue is who controls what is relevant to the results regarding feasibility. The crop grower chooses what to grow; school leaders do not choose who attends their schools. This difference in the degree of control might explain why the majority of the school leaders disagree with the feasibility of these two recommendations.

Should these results and the reasons given for them cause us to dismiss the crop grower's recommendations altogether? We do not think so because there is a lesson here. The lesson is about the school leader who has usually been viewed as a generalist. But in relationship to school accountability, the teaching staff might in fact view the principal as a specialist.

The crop grower works with ranch managers who are generalists, engaging in planning of schedules, attending to crop growth, and evaluating results. He cannot do without them. The ranch managers view their ranch as their own, even though they do not make final decisions on what to grow. But when managers encounter growth problems, they turn to the specialist.

Likewise, the school principal works with teachers who are also generalists engaging in planning lessons, instructing students, and evaluating learning. The school leader cannot do without them. But when they encounter learning problems, teachers turn to the principal. The principal is the specialist with regard to reducing interference with learning.

In both cases, it is a coordinated effort, but ultimately, it is the responsibility of the leader who has to remain accountable. When crop growth interference occurs, ranch managers turn to the grower for maintaining crop growth accountability. And when learning problems occur, teachers turn to the principal for ways to improve student learning.

CHALLENGE 4—SOLVING PROBLEMS

The automobile service advisor made three recommendations to school leaders in relationship to problem-solving competencies. His first recommendation was to spend time reflecting about a solution to a problem and about how to communicate it.

A large majority of the surveyed school leaders saw this as useful. Two-thirds of them felt that it was feasible. Most of the rest of the respondents actually said that they needed help in improving their interpersonal skills with regard to communicating problems to others. "Need training," one said. Another said, "You need to learn how to do it." It behooves school districts to respond to this need, possibly allowing for "residency" time with the automobile service advisor. Shadowing him and discussing what was observed might help in identifying how to handle simultaneously existing problems at different stages of solution.

Somewhat less of but still a significant majority found the second recommendation (namely, improving the ability to market the school) as useful. One secondary school principal said, "This is the most important task." Another said, "Accountability calls for it." With regard to the feasibility of improving the ability to market the school, almost all of those who wrote "useful" also wrote "feasible." Those who said "yes" to feasibility made useful suggestions: "Simply describe what you do daily; that is selling." "Work with PTA." "Increase the school visibility. How about a website"? "Advertise student performance." "Celebrate student accomplishments."

Such examples constitute food for thought for those practitioners who are reluctant to see this recommendation as useful. One reluctant respondent wrote, "The location of some schools gives them a bad image no matter what you say." Another said, "You cannot control the media." These practitioners may be right. But their own colleagues have ideas for improving the marketing of their school. Principals who are good marketers often point to their school's record of problem solving as a marketing tool.

The third recommendation related to the challenge of solving problems (namely, making decisions more from the heart than what is now done) produced a mixed bag of responses. Few in the secondary schools but more in the elementary schools said "yes" to the usefulness of this recommendation. Why is there a difference? Does the age of the students make a difference? Is it less illegal and easier to hug a second grader than a tenth grader? Does a reaction from the heart have a stronger effect on a second grader than on a tenth grader?

Respondents who argued against this recommendation raised issues about legalities, policies, school rules, consistency, and the school's culture. Other specific reasons for disagreeing with this recommendation included avoidance of personalizing, negative effects of expressing emotions, and problems with being impulsive.

But the message that the automobile service advisor wished to give with this recommendation was not to replace decisions from the mind with decisions from the heart. Rather, he called for not totally avoiding the latter. It is especially those school leaders who deal with children who may not have been treated much "from the heart" and who might wish to consider the automobile service advisor's suggestion seriously. Leader accountability also involves treating youngsters with empathy.

One secondary school principal wrote, "I must run a school as a business with its philosophy and culture." To him the service advisor might have responded, "That does not exclude having respect and care for individuals." School leaders need to become specialists in using their hearts in decision making. They should also know where the need for "using the heart" should stop and "using the head" should become paramount.

CHALLENGE 5—FIDUCIARY RESPONSIBILITY

Approximately 80 percent of the respondents saw the CFO's sole recommendation regarding taking fiduciary responsibility as useful. The recommendation was to acquire budgetary knowledge over and above simple accounting and auditing skills. It included learning about the budgets and their contexts.

Respondents reacted to the feasibility of this recommendation as follows: secondary school principals asked for additional training in fiscal matters, more than elementary school principals did. The larger size of the discretionary budget per student at the secondary level might explain this request. Several of those who asked for help in acquiring additional skills also asked that the district offer it (in house) or else pay for them to take courses outside.

CHALLENGE 6—PROVIDING COMFORT

The hospital chaplain made two recommendations to school leaders about providing comfort to those in pain and to those who have been punished: "Improve your intuitive, spontaneous, and communicative skills," and "love people, learning, and teaching." An overwhelming number of secondary school leaders and a smaller majority of the elementary school leaders saw both recommendations as useful. Smaller proportions of respondents said "yes" to the feasibility of these two recommendations.

Most of those who said that it would not be feasible to implement these recommendations also asked for help to do so. One respondent wrote, "If you don't have such skills, you need to work on them." Another said, "You have got to watch what you say. That is difficult sometimes." A third pointed out, "How can I teach these things if I need to learn them myself?" Three respondents who wrote "maybe" asked for staff development in this area for themselves.

A large majority of school leaders are probably anxious to provide comfort when needed. If anything is lacking in this area, it is in their current capacity to do so. Acquiring this ability may be easier than following the advice of the automobile service advisor about acting more from the heart than the head.

In helping to solve a problem, a balance is needed between mind and heart because the problem needs to be solved (a clear and specific objective). In providing comfort and emotional support, the balance might tilt almost all the way to the heart. The objective is to instill hope (any measure of hope is beneficial).

The question is how to increase the capacity of school leaders who wish to provide solace when needed. Specialists such as a hospital chaplain might help in this regard. Should school leaders do residency with a hospital chaplain? We are not sure.

CHALLENGE 7—MANAGING AND ADJUDICATING CONFLICTS

The courtroom judge spends most of her time managing and adjudicating conflicts. Her three recommendations to school leaders amounted to a behavioral menu in handling conflict. Overwhelming majorities of the surveyed school leaders saw the three recommendations (namely, maximizing knowledge about a conflict before getting involved in it, turning the conflict into problems to be solved by amicable means, and providing a model behavior for others to follow) as useful.

Feasibility was perceived as less likely. "Time" was an issue about the first recommendation (learning about the case ahead of time). With regard to the other two recommendations (turning conflicts into problems to be solved amicably and modeling behavior), several respondents provided ways of actually implementing them. This might imply that these school leaders already know what it takes to manage and adjudicate in school. They probably resolve conflicts without help. Those who might wish to improve these specialized competencies could ask for professional development in learning and practicing what they need to know in this area.

CHALLENGE 8—USING STUDENT ACHIEVEMENT DATA TO BENEFIT FUTURE PERFORMANCE

The choral conductor made two fundamental recommendations to practicing school leaders. Both recommendations contained suggestions about ways of making beneficial use of the information from student achievement test scores. The first recommendation included praising the achievement and becoming a strong and charismatic advocate of the school's achievements. He also called for interpreting the meaning of the student test scores to different audiences with the hope of strengthening the sense of ownership of the school by these audiences.

Only one secondary school leader did not see this recommendation as useful. "Media can be misleading," the person wrote. That may be true. Also, only one elementary school leader saw no use for the recommendation. The reason given was that "charisma is not the most important quality." It may not be. As to feasibility, about half of the respondents did not feel that it is possible to implement this recommendation.

It could very well be that the mention of "charisma" by the choral conductor bothered them, or at least some of them (fifteen mentioned charisma in their reasons). Examples included the following: "It is a gift." "It is not teachable." "Not everyone is highly charismatic." Of the twelve elementary school respondents who did not agree with this recommendation, three mentioned charisma.

Several respondents offered ways of reaching out to the stakeholders: "Use data and public relations." "If you believe in it, you can promote it." "Hit the correct people." So some school leaders know how to do it, and they do it despite the fact that it takes much planning and presentation time. It is even harder to accomplish when the students' scores are low.

Some school leaders probably do not do it because of lack of time, lack of willingness, lack of ability, an unsuitable personality, or a low sense of efficacy. Time could be better managed. Efficacy could be improved. In order to increase leader accountability it might help to offer a "residency" with a specialist who can show how to praise outcome data, explaining their meaning in ways that are beneficial to the school.

Some school leaders might also need to learn how to analyze test scores in order to guide teachers in improving their instruction of their students. Again, an overwhelming majority of the school leaders found this recommendation (the second one offered by the chorus conductor) useful. There was only one "no" answer. A few of the respondents did not see the recommendation as feasible—more among elementary than among secondary school leaders. Why? "Need training," said several of them.

"Learn to use tools to understand the data and how these data should drive decisions in schools," wrote one. "Communicate with the district on the need to learn," wrote another. Professional evaluators might be of help here. They can explain how to read actual achievement test scores, how to interpret them in relationship to the learner's strengths and weaknesses, and also suggest possible changes in instructional methods and objectives. They can also help in showing how to monitor subsequent scores and make further instructional adjustments. This would constitute a major step toward improving leadership accountability.

16

When, Where, and How to Acquire and Use the Special Competencies

School leadership has been considered a generalist profession. One reason for this is that school leaders are trained to interact with not one but a variety of educational specialists and others specialists who work with the educators. Among these people are classroom teachers, school psychologists and counselors, office and plant managers, and government and finance officials. School leaders also interact with politicians and public service officials, businesspeople, industrialists, clergy, and leaders of other nonprofit organizations.

Introductory textbooks of school administration and leadership are organized according to various fields. Several published research and scholarly works pertaining to school administration and leadership are anchored in corresponding working assumptions and theories. These include publications about school leadership and learning, instruction, individual differences, organizations, management, politics, and economics.

Because of additional and varied needs that today's pupils have and because the fulfillment of these needs is increasingly perceived through eyes that are focused on accountability, the view that school leadership is a generalist profession is no longer valid. In this spirit, this book has taken on a postgeneralist conceptual view of school leadership as it relates to accountability. Simply put, schooling today and in the days to come requires leadership that possesses knowledge and skills in many specific areas.

Accordingly, this book identified specific school-leadership challenges that are associated with today's intensified calls for accountability in schools. Given the assumption that facing each of these specific challenges would require a set of specialized competencies, our research sought possible competencies. We identified some of these competencies during conversations with specialists, each of whose full-time occupation is focused on a comparable challenge faced by school leaders.

Next we discussed our preliminary check of how useful and how feasible some school practitioners perceive these competencies to be. This last chapter of the book will offer some suggestions related to the acquisition and use of these specialized competencies. According to our theory, acquiring and using these specialized competencies in meeting the eight challenges would allow school leaders to become more accountable.

But first, there is a need to revisit the accountability-related leadership challenges that were chosen for the book and that require specialized competencies in order to meet them. Earlier we noted that our eight choices stemmed from our accumulated experience in the field of education and that we were not the first writers to identify them.

Some writers have dealt with one or two of these major challenges. For example, in reading Hoyle's (2002) work on the force of love in leadership, one sees a clear relationship to our challenge 6 (providing comfort). The work of Ortony, Clore, and Collins (1988) and the work of Yukl (2002) on the cognitive structure of emotions also relates to this challenge. The writing of Goleman, Boyatzis, and McKee (2002) discusses the notion of expressions of empathy as part of emotional leadership. Empathy is one of the pivotal dimensions of emotional leadership and, therefore, it closely resembles some of the specialized competencies that are needed to meet challenge 6.

Beaudoin and Taylor (2004), Lee (2004), Moeller (2001), O'Moore and Minton (2004), and Sullivan, Cleary, and Sullivan (2004) have all written about bullying in schools and how the school leader's presence could minimize it. This relates to our challenge 2, patrolling the school grounds for safety and rule enforcement. Also related to this challenge is the work of Burstyn et al. (2001) on school violence and the work of Fishbaugh, Schroth, and Berkeley (2003) on school safety. Dealing with difficult parents (Jaksec 2005) and troubled teachers (McEwan 2005) is also related to challenge 2. Imber and Van Geel (1993) have presented an overview of student rights that involves other dimensions of our challenge 2.

Daresh (2001) has focused on issues related to school goals, similar to our challenge 1. Spillane and Orlina (2005) and Weick (1976) have written on how, respectively, the leadership and the organization need to be structured to achieve these goals. Johnson (2002) concentrated on how using student achievement data may help close the achievement gap. Ward and Burke (2004) have edited a volume devoted to adjusting teaching in accord with student performance. These works relate to challenge 8.

All of this literature, however, is not necessarily designed to show that these individual challenges are part of the larger issue of school-leadership accountability. Of course, there is also literature that deals with school-leadership accountability in general (Cooley and Shen 1999; Reeves 2002). But such writing does not spell out specific challenges that school leaders face when their accountability is on the line.

Respectively, then, these two areas of literature represent either specific problems that leaders face but are not necessarily related to accountability, or leadership accountability that is not necessarily related to facing challenges. We have tried to address both of these issues and to expand the knowledge base about the profession of school leadership that embodies specific accountability demands. Indeed, we hope that this challenge-based school-leadership approach will help practitioners become more proactive by reframing and more widely publicizing the authentic responses that they make to calls for their accountability. Clearly this is only a beginning.

At this point, a preliminary list of the needed specialized competencies is offered. The list is based on the recommendations offered by the specialists and on our general analysis of the reactions to them made by some practicing school leaders.

1. Achieving predetermined school goals

    - Acquiring leadership experience alongside a practicing school leader
    - Learning why and how to integrate a new staff member into the team
    - Developing the abilities to both assume responsibility for problems and to communicate these problems effectively to others
    - Learning how to act in problematic situations according to the priorities of safety, comfort, learning schedule, and efficiency
    - Developing self-confidence in times when decisions must be made autonomously

2. Maintaining safety and rule enforcement

    - Identifying useful purposes for patrolling the school ground as well as target locations, best times to patrol, useful approaches, and types of interactions while patrolling, and identifying and training individuals who can also assume this task
    - Developing comfort in acting from a position of authority when necessary
    - Learning ways to collaborate with other agencies when needed while minimizing confusion about each person's responsibilities
    - Learning how to help teachers act from a position of authority
    - Learning to interact effectively with law-enforcement personnel when they are on campus
    - Practicing interpretations and prompt applications of school district policies and rules

3. Enhancing outcomes of student learning

   - Learning to diagnose learning problems and acting collaboratively, decisively, and efficiently to minimize these interferences with learning
   - Practicing the three interrelated activities associated with curriculum: developing it on the basis of district guidelines, implementing it, and conducting the testing programs to determine if the learning fundamentals required for future job and higher education success have been attained

4. Problem solving

   - Learning the value of and how to reflect effectively in problematic situations in order to make and communicate effective decisions
   - Developing and using strategies for marketing the school
   - Engaging in self-teaching in order to improve decision making "from the heart," when appropriate, and improving in ways of communicating these decisions

5. Assuming fiduciary responsibility

   - Learning how budgets and their contextual forces operate, with a focus on efficiency and minimization of accounting errors

6. Providing comfort when needed

   - Practicing the use of intuition, spontaneity, and communication skills
   - Developing a greater love of people, learning, and teaching

7. Managing and adjudicating conflicts

   - Learning to gather the information related to a conflict in a minimum amount of time and before getting involved in the conflict
   - Practicing ways to turn a conflict into a set of problems to be solved by amicable means
   - Learning to behave in an exemplary way (modeling)

8. Using student achievement data in beneficial ways

   - Learning to praise student achievement with the dual aims of increasing student morale and expanding a sense of ownership by stakeholders
   - Learning to analyze student achievement test scores and practicing working with teachers to improve instruction by using this information

We move now to the question of what are the best times for the acquisition of the various sets of specialized competencies listed above. Our answer is based on the following four criteria:

1. Those in school-leadership positions are expected to be accountable for each challenge at the time in their career that is appropriate to their experience.
2. The acquisition of some competencies is a prerequisite to the acquisition of other competencies.
3. By the time those in school-leadership positions need to be accountable for a particular challenge, they must have acquired all of the competencies required to face and meet this challenge.
4. And there are five distinct periods of time in the career trajectory of a future school leader or a practicing school leader:

   - the academic portion of preparation (trainee);
   - a school-leadership internship (intern);
   - an assistant principalship (AP);
   - the first few years of one's principalship (novice); and
   - the career of a principal after the first few years on the job (experienced)

On the basis of these criteria, we now present our answer to the question about the appropriate times during which we believe the twenty-four sets of specialized competencies should be acquired. First, we present the information in the table 16.1. This is followed by a detailed discussion of each set of competencies and the proper time for its acquisition, as well as the manner in which it might be acquired. Again, the challenges are as follows:

1. Achieving goals
2. Safety issues
3. Problem solving
4. Producing outcomes
5. Fiduciary responsibility
6. Offering comfort
7. Managing conflicts
8. Using data

Starting with the academic leadership preparatory program, there are five competencies that constitute prerequisites to other competencies. Three of them include learning how to integrate new staff members, assuming responsibility, and reflecting about decisions and how to communicate them (Fullan 2005). These competencies make up an important part of the leadership infrastructure. The earlier they are developed, the stronger the leadership foundation will turn out to be because they involve interpersonal relations (Gardner 1983).

Not many leadership preparatory programs include teaching concepts and, more importantly, devising opportunities for skill development in relation to

Table 16.1.   Suggested Timetable for Acquiring Competencies

Time Period	Competencies to be Acquired
Trainee	Integration of staff (2), Responsibility for problems (3), Reflection about decisions (14), Diagnosis of learning problems (12), Evaluation of test results (24)
Intern	Priorities in problematic situations (4), Patrolling with a principal (6)
Assistant Principal	Practice alongside a principal (1), Law enforcement (10), Interpreting policies (11), Intuition (18)
Novice	Self-confidence with autonomy (5), Collaboration (8), Curriculum (13), Budget (17), Love (19), Conflict information (20), Amicable means (21)
Experienced	Comfort with authority (7), Teachers' comfort with authority (9), Marketing the school (15), Decisions from the heart (16), Modeling behavior (22), Praise and interpret data (23)

these specialized competencies (Cunningham and Cordeiro 2006); Lunenburg and Ornstein 2003). Not many professors who teach in leadership-preparation programs are clinically qualified to train their students in these areas.

Two other specialized competencies that are generally absent from the academic portion of preparatory programs are diagnosing learning difficulties and evaluating student achievement test scores for instructional improvement. Both are interrelated prerequisites, needed later by principals in conjunction with other competencies in working on cognitive development and student achievement with students, teachers, and parents. The corresponding material must be studied in the university or college classroom with qualified program evaluators.

Learning how to set priorities during emergency times (putting safety first) and how to conceptualize and practice the maintenance of safety by patrolling the school grounds ought to be acquired during the internship portion of the preparation program. Together, interns, school supervisors, and university clinicians could plan specific experiences for interns to which they could be exposed and upon which they would reflect.

Specialized competency 1 would be attained by serving as an assistant principal. The literature on the assistant principalship is expanding (Daresh 2004). One reason is that practitioners realize how helpful and necessary this school-leadership position is. Another reason is that scholars and researchers are still trying to understand what assistant principals really do and how they can significantly enhance their contribution to the school while improving their own skills and knowledge.

Three additional specialized competencies could best be acquired during the assistant principalship. These three competencies include (1) learning to interact effectively with law-enforcement personnel; (2) practicing the interpretation and application of school district policies; and (3) developing intuitiveness and spontaneity in order to improve communication skills.

When these competencies are acquired under the mentorship of the school principal, assistant principals can rest assured that their decisions will most likely be backed up by the principal. In the event that they experience difficulties making decisions, they may consult with the principal or rely on the principal to assume responsibility for making those decisions. Assistant principals not only engage in certain activities themselves but also have opportunities to observe how the principal behaves. Then they can discuss what they see with the principal and ask for explanations and rationale.

So far there has not been any detailed discussion of accountability because a school leader's accountability does not begin until the first day on the job as a principal. Eleven specialized competencies have been discussed so far. Development of the other specialized competencies should take place in the novice period and the experienced period.

Of the thirteen specialized competencies not yet discussed in this chapter, seven of them should be acquired as early as possible in the school leader's career, possibly within three or so years from the first day on the job as principal. The other six competencies could be acquired somewhat later, because no school leader should be held totally accountable prior to having some actual experience.

No matter how new a principal might be on the job, she or he already faces some of the challenges we introduced in this book:

- achieving goals, with the specialized competency of developing self-confidence in the context of autonomous decision making (5);
- assuring safety and rule enforcement, with the specialized competency of coordinating and minimizing confusion (8);
- enhancing student-learning outcomes, with the competency of developing curriculum (13);
- being fiscally responsible, with the specialized competency of understanding the budgetary context and enhancing efficiency (17);
- providing comfort, with the specialized competency of showing care and compassion (19);
- managing and adjudicating conflicts, with the specialized competencies of learning about a conflict (20); and
- turning the conflict into problems to be solved by amicable means (21).

Within no more than one year on the job, novice school leaders could begin to engage in pursuing these challenges, not just for doing their job but also with an eye toward becoming as accountable as possible. They may ask themselves, how well am I doing in acquiring and using the specialized competencies that I need in order to pursue as effectively as I can the particular challenges that I face and for which I stand accountable?

Self-confidence may be self-taught, practiced, and assessed. The district office could provide coaching about cooperative leadership. Removing interferences to student learning must be done with the complete participation of the teachers and other professionals in the school. The district should sponsor professional-development activities about budgetary matters. Concern for others should be acquired over the course of time. Conflict management might be self-taught or introduced via interactive seminars or classes.

As principals gain experience (Wilmore 2004) they can expand their efforts to face other challenges while acquiring the rest of the specialized competencies:

- providing safety, with the specialized competencies of being comfortable in acting from a position of authority (7) and helping teachers act from a position of authority (9);
- solving problems, with the specialized competencies of marketing (15) and deciding from the heart (16);
- conflict resolution, with the specialized competency of modeling behavior (22); and
- making beneficial uses of achievement results, with the special competency of both praising achievement and interpreting test scores for other stakeholders (23).

Self-teaching could be one way of acquiring the following specialized competencies: developing comfort to act from a position of authority, helping teachers to do the same, improving the making of decisions from the heart, and increasing the capacity to behave as a model for others. Mastering the specialized competency of marketing and expanding ownership of results would probably require the help of marketing experts and public-relations professionals.

In summary, only three challenges directly involve student learning and teacher instruction (achieving goals, assuring growth, and using test results). The other challenges involve improving the milieu within which learning and instruction take place (assuring safety, solving problems, dealing with finances, providing comfort, and managing conflicts). On the whole, these two types of challenges require different specialized competencies, but all eight of them need to be met before an experienced principal can be a school leader who is accountable to all of her or his stakeholders (Firestone and Shipps 2005).

It behooves experienced school leaders to take an active part in helping less-experienced leaders to improve their accountability if there is a need for it and if the less-experienced leader is willing to be coached (Daresh 2001). This may be done with regard to the pursuit of any one or more of the eight specialized challenges and with regard to any one or more of the twenty-four specialized competencies.

Over the years, we have met many not-so-experienced principals who are working very hard to improve their accountability as school leaders. Experienced principals might even detect a thing or two that they can learn from less-experienced principals.

In this book, accountability has been considered an integral part of leadership. We believe that there can be no leadership without accountability. As we conclude this book, we must state what we believe to be another axiom: there is no accountability without evaluation.

In its most general form, evaluation is the gathering of information and the rendering of judgment about its merit. For our purposes we see evaluation as enabling stakeholders of schools and school leaders themselves to better identify and measure accountability beyond simply stating that "accountability exists, and we are working to improve it." It is beyond the scope of this book to present even an introduction to evaluating school-leadership accountability as a function of meeting the challenges.

So we close by saying this: throughout the career of a school leader, specialized competencies must be acquired and used, and their use must be evaluated from two perspectives. One perspective uses a formative approach where performance is assessed and the results are used for improvement. The other perspective uses a summative approach in which the extent of the use of the specialized competencies is assessed (Stufflebeam et al. 1988).

The summative approach is accountability driven. We strongly recommend that it be done as a measure of the success in pursuing each of the eight challenges described in this book. Rejecting our or similar types of suggestions might be interpreted as holding the position that it is totally impossible to reduce some of the vagueness associated with defining school-leadership accountability. It is simply no longer acceptable to leave school-leadership accountability as a vague concept or practice.

Epilogue

This book has been a journey that began with considering demands for educational accountability that are placed on school leaders and ended with pointing out the importance of an evaluation process to assess how accountable school leaders have become.

Specific demands represent themselves as specific leadership challenges. The pursuit of the challenges calls for the acquisition and use of specialized competencies. Various professionals offered recommendations about these specialized competencies. Actual school leaders then provided opinions about the usefulness and feasibility of these recommendations. The journey continued with suggestions about (1) times during the career of future leaders and practicing leaders in which the specialized competencies ought to be acquired and (2) some examples of sources and ways of acquiring these specialized competencies.

Now we need to state some disclaimers. No systematic attempt was made in this book to cover what we know about school leadership (e.g., Leithwood and Riehl 2005, chapter 2). Ours is a book on leadership accountability, how to attain it and how to improve it with the aid of specialized lenses.

Consider this. Late in 2005, the Council of the Great City Schools (a body that serves as a national voice for sixty-six large urban school districts) issued a report dealing with accountability issues in the Los Angeles Unified School District, the nation's second-largest district. The report found a lack of accountability at almost all levels of the district. It pointed out that some goals have been developed but that there is confusion about who is accountable to whom, for which goal, and in what ways.

The report singled out school leaders, including teachers, as highly confused in this regard. Our book pays only scant attention to teachers. The reason for this is not that school leaders can improve their accountability without the assistance of teachers; they cannot. Teacher accountability is certainly a highly related topic (Bridges 1992; Brimley and Garfield 2002; Espelage and Swearer 2004). But that is simply outside of the scope of this book.

Throughout the book we mention only a few examples and implications of student, teacher, and leader diversity in relation to accountability (Connerley and Pedersen 2005). Diversity affects the intensity and boundaries of the leader's challenges and the leader's inclination to acquire specialized competencies.

We deliberated about the significance of color, gender, ethnicity, age (Glasman and DelVecchio 2004, chapter 12), and psychological mindset (Branden 1994; Seligman 1990) and their association with a leader's approach to accountability. But we realize this topic calls for additional research, so we did not include a discussion of it here.

Since the early 1950s, numerous students of leadership have viewed the process as involving the leader's rational exercise of power to attain a goal (task orientation) and the leader's sensitivity to the welfare of the followers while the goal is being pursued (consideration). Scholars have often written about the need to strike a balance between the two (Enns and Huff 1997; Nanus 1989; Torbert 1991). In this book, we wrestled with this dilemma as well but did not come to a resolution regarding the optimal balance.

The context of the information-technology age was not mentioned in the book. This is so despite our belief that school-leadership accountability could improve with the improvement of information flow in and around the school (Kent 2000). But at this point we do not know enough about how professional knowledge moves among people and how this movement is managed in the school (Lakomski 2005). This topic also deserves further study.

Most importantly, we now call upon those with the power to do so to find ways that would help current school leaders to become more accountable. They need this help. Clear priorities here include improving accountability, being comfortable with its improvement, effectively managing the improvement, and also being proud of the improvement. These actions and behaviors will help the school leader develop a highly prized organizational image for the school (Morgan 1986). Accountability of school leaders is also a matter of image, not just substance. And it cannot replace meeting challenges with specialized competencies.

References

Beaudoin, M., and M. Taylor. 2004. *Breaking the culture of bullying and disrespect, grades K–8*. Thousand Oaks, Calif.: Corwin.

Beckwith, H. 2003. *What clients love*. New York: Warner Books.

Bennis, W., and B. Nanus. 1985. *Leaders: The strategies for taking charge*. New York: Harper & Row.

Boyan, N., ed. 1988. *Handbook of research on educational administration*. New York: Longman.

Branden, N. 1994. *The six pillars of self-esteem*. New York: Bantam.

Brealey, R. A., and S. C. Myers. 2003. *Principles of corporate finance*. Boston: McGraw-Hill.

Bridges, E. 1992. *The incompetent teacher*. Washington, D.C.: Falmer.

Brimley, V. Jr., and R. R. Garfield. 2002. *Financing education in a climate of change*. Boston: Allyn and Bacon.

Browder, L. H., ed. 1971. *Emerging patterns of administrative accountability*. Berkley, Calif.: McCutchan.

Burstyn, J. N., et al. 2001. *Preventing violence in schools*. Mahwah, N.J.: L. Erlbaum Associates.

Connerley, M. L., and P. B. Pedersen. 2005. *Leadership in a diverse and multicultural environment*. Thousand Oaks, Calif.: Sage.

Cooley, V. E., and J. Shen. 1999. School accountability and principals' professional job responsibilities. In *School Principals*, ed. J. Shen. New York: P. Lang.

Cousins, N. 1983. *The healing heart*. New York: W. W. Norton.

Cunningham, W. G., and P. A. Cordeiro. 2006. *Educational leadership*. Boston: Allyn and Bacon.

Daresh, J. C. 2001. *Leaders helping leaders*. Thousand Oaks, Calif.: Corwin.

——. 2004. *Beginning the assistant principalship*. Thousand Oaks, Calif.: Corwin.

Davis, S., L. Darling-Hammond, M. Lapointe, and D. Meyerson. 2005. *School leadership study: Developing successful principals*. Stanford, Calif.: Stanford Educational Leadership Institute.

Duke, D. 2004. *The challenges of educational change.* Boston: Allyn and Bacon.

Duke, D., M. Grogen, and P. Tucker. 2003. Educational leadership in the age of accountability. In *Educational leadership in an age of accountability,* ed. D. Duke, M. Grogen, and P. Tucker. Albany: State University of New York Press.

Enns, H., and S. Huff. 1997. CIO's influence on business strategy formulation and realization. Power and politics organization theory. Houston, Tex.: Baylor University.

Espelage, D. L., and S. M. Swearer. 2004. *Bullying in American schools.* Mahwah, N.J.: L. Erlbaum Associates.

Firestone, W. A., and D. Shipps. 2005. How do leaders interpret conflicting accountabilities to improve student learning? In *A new agenda for research in educational leadership,* ed. W. A. Firestone and C. Riehl, chap. 6. New York: Teachers College Press.

Fishbaugh, M. S. E., G. Schroth, and T. R. Berkeley, eds. 2003. *Ensuring safe school environments.* Mahwah, N.J.: L. Erlbaum Associates.

Fullan, M. 2005. *Leadership & sustainability: System thinkers in action.* Thousand Oaks, Calif.: Corwin.

Gardner, H. 1983. *Frames of mind: The theory of multiple intelligences.* New York: Basic Books.

Gergen, D. 2000. *Eyewitness to power.* New York: Simon & Schuster.

Glasman, N. S. 1994. *Making better decisions about school problems.* Thousand Oaks, Calif.: Corwin.

———. 2002. Recasting educational leadership preparation programs (guest editor). *Leadership and Policy in Schools* 1 (3): 284–85.

Glasman, N. S., J. Cibulka, and D. Ashby. 2002. Program self-evaluation for continuous improvement. *Educational Administration Quarterly* 38 (2): 257–88.

Glasman N. S., and R. L. Crowson. 1998. Reexamining relations and the sense of place between schools and their constituents. *Peabody Journal of Education* 76 (2): 1–8.

Glasman, N. S., and V. DelVecchio. 2004. *Leadership for the rest of us.* Solvang, Calif.: Reference Desk Books.

Glasman, N. S., and R. Heck. 1992/1993. New ways of assessing the performance of school principals, parts I and II (guest editors). *Peabody Journal of Education* 68 (1, 2).

Glasman, N. S., R. Koff, and H. Spiers. 1980. Reasoning and education. *Review of Educational Research, Special Issue* 54 (4): 461–695.

Glasman, N. S., and D. Nevo. 1988. *Evaluation in decision making.* Boston: Kluwer.

Goleman, D., R. Boyatzis, and A. McKee. 2002. *Primal leadership: Realizing the power of emotional intelligence.* Boston: Harvard Business School Press.

Green, R. L. 2005. *Practicing the art of leadership.* Upper Saddle River, N.J.: Pearson.

Greenberg, J., and R. Baron. 2000. *Behavior in organizations.* Upper Saddle River, N.J.: Prentice Hall.

Hemphill, J., and A. Coons. 1955. Development of the leader behavior description questionnaire. In *Leader behavior,* ed. R. Stogdill and A. Coons. Columbus: Ohio State University Press.

Hess, F. P., and A. P. Kelly. 2005a. *Learning to lead* (FEPG 05-02). Washington, D.C.: American Enterprise Institute.

———. 2005b. *Textbook learning* (FEPG 05-03). Washington, D.C.: American Enterprise Institute.

Hoyle, J. R. 2002. *Leadership and the force of love.* Thousand Oaks, Calif.: Corwin.

Imber, M., and T. van Geel. 1993. *Education law.* New York: McGraw-Hill.

Jaksec, C. M. 2005. *The difficult parent.* Thousand Oaks, Calif.: Corwin.

Johnson, R. S. 2002. *Using data to close the achievement gap.* Thousand Oaks, Calif.: Corwin.

Kent, R. E. 2000. The information flow foundation for conceptual knowledge organization. The 6th International Conference of the International Society for Knowledge Organization, Toronto.

Lakomski, G. 2005. *Managing without leadership.* Amsterdam, the Netherlands: Elsevier.

Lee, C. 2004. *Preventing bullying in schools.* Thousand Oaks, Calif.: Sage.

Leithwood, K., and D. Duke. 1999. A century's quest to understand school leadership. In *Handbook of research on educational administration,* ed. J. Murphy and L. K. Seashore, 45–72. San Francisco: Jossey-Bass.

Leithwood, K., and C. Riehl. 2005. What do we already know about educational leadership? In *A new agenda for research in educational leadership,* ed. W. A. Firestone and C. Riehl, chap. 2. New York: Teachers College Press.

Lunenburg, F. C., and A. C. Ornstein. 2003. *Educational administration.* Belmont, Calif.: Wadsworth.

McEwan, E. K. 2005. *How to deal with teachers who are angry, troubled, exhausted, or just plain confused.* Thousand Oaks, Calif.: Corwin.

Milstein, M. 1993. *Changing the way we prepare educational leaders: The Danforth experience.* Newbury Park, Calif.: Corwin.

Moeller, T. G. 2001. *Youth aggression and violence.* Mahwah, N.J.: L. Erlbaum Associates.

Morgan, G. 1986. *Images of organization.* Beverly Hills, Calif.: Sage.

Murphy, J., and M. Vriesenga. 2004. *Research on preparation programs in educational administration: An analysis.* Columbia: University Council for Educational Administration, University of Missouri, Columbia.

Nanus, B. 1989. *The leader's edge.* Chicago: Contemporary Books.

O'Moore, M., and S. J. Minton. 2004. *Dealing with bullying in schools.* Thousand Oaks, Calif.: Sage.

Ortony, A., G. L. Clore, and A. Collins. 1988. *The Cognitive structure of emotions.* Cambridge, UK: Cambridge University Press.

Reeves, D. B. 2002. *Holistic accountability.* Thousand Oaks, Calif.: Corwin.

Robbins, P., and H. B. Alvy. 2003. *The principal's companion.* Thousand Oaks, Calif.: Corwin.

Seligman, M. E. P. 1990. *Learned optimism.* New York: Pocket Books.

Spillane, J. P., and E. C. Orlina. 2005. Investigating leadership practice: Exploring the entailments of taking a distributive perspective. *Leadership and Policy in Schools* 4 (3): 157–76.

Starratt, R. J. 2003. *Centering educational administration.* Mahwah, N.J.: L. Erlbaum Associates.

Stufflebeam, D., et al. 1988. *The personnel evaluation standards.* Newbury Park, Calif.: Sage.

Sullivan, K., M. Cleary, and G. Sullivan. 2004. *Bullying in secondary schools.* Thousand Oaks, Calif.: Corwin.

Torbert, W. R. 1991. *The power of balance.* Newbury Park, Calif.: Sage.

Vuillemainroy, R. L. 2004. School violence and crisis response: Evaluating a next step. PhD diss., University of California, Santa Barbara.

Ward, R. E., and M. A. Burke, eds. 2004. *Improving achievement in low-performing schools*. Thousand Oaks, Calif.: Corwin.

Weick, K. E. 1976. Educational organizations as loosely coupled systems. *Administrative Science Quarterly* 21 (1): 1–19.

Wilmore, E. L. 2004. *Principal induction*. Thousand Oaks, Calif.: Corwin.

Young, M. D., G. J. Petersen, and P. M. Short. 2002. The complexity of substantive reform. *Educational Administration Quarterly* 38 (2): 136–75.

Yukl, G. A. 2002. *Leadership in organizations*. Upper Saddle River, N.J.: Prentice Hall.

About the Authors

Naftaly S. Glasman and Lynette D. Glasman both received their PhD degrees from the University of California, Berkeley, in 1968, he in educational administration and she in educational psychology. Prior to 1968, they taught and administered schools, Naftaly (Tuli) at the secondary level and Lynette (Lynne) at the elementary level. They both began work at the University of California, Santa Barbara (UCSB), in 1968, he in the Graduate School of Education and she in the Department of Psychology.

During the 1980s, Tuli served as the dean of the UCSB Graduate School of Education. He later taught as a visiting professor at UCLA and also in four Israeli universities. Currently he is in his thirty-eighth year at the University of California, Santa Barbara.

In addition to teaching at UCSB, Lynne has taught in other colleges and served as a consultant and researcher in California and Israel. She has published journal articles and book chapters on program evaluation, cognitive development, and bilingual education. In addition, she has worked with district and county education offices as an evaluation consultant and written proposals for several social service agencies, proposals that were generously funded by government and private agencies.

Tuli served as associate editor and editor of the *Review of Educational Research*, a journal published by the American Association of Educational Research. He has over 160 publications. These publications include journal articles, book chapters, books, and monographs. Among the publications are

- "Reasoning and Education," *Review of Educational Research* (coeditor with Robert Koff)
- *Evaluation-Based Leadership* (author)

- "New Ways to Assess the Performance of School Principals," *Peabody Journal of Education* (coeditor with Ronald Heck)
- *Evaluation in Decision Making* (coauthor with David Nevo)
- *Making Better Decisions about School Problems* (author)
- "Reexamining Relations and a Sense of Place between Schools and Their Constituents," *Peabody Journal of Education* (coeditor with Robert Crowson)
- "Recasting Educational Leadership Preparation Programs," *Journal of School Policy and Leadership* (editor)

The Glasmans live in Santa Barbara. They have three children and four grandchildren.

CPSIA information can be obtained at www.ICGtesting.com
Printed in the USA
LVOW012139281011

252621LV00006B/59/P